Endorse

"Egalitarian and chauvinistic thinking have corrupted our ideas about godly manhood. With boldness of heart and pastoral wisdom, Rick Phillips leads us back toward biblical manhood—masculinity grounded in the cultural mandate, the cross, and the ordinary means of grace. May men of the church answer the call of this mandate to stand up and be counted, and to live out their faith courageously as workers, protectors, nurturers, and leaders for Christ."

—*Eric C. Redmond*
Professor of Bible
Moody Bible Institute, Chicago
Author, *Where Are All the Brothers?*
Straight Answers to Men's Questions about the Church

"In the face of the widespread confusion in our culture, Rick Phillips lays out the biblical mandate for men to work and keep the world around us. This book carefully avoids stereotypes and legalistic rules, while unfolding with clarity and practical simplicity the biblical vision of men as individuals and in relationships to other men, to our wives and children, and to the church of Jesus Christ. I learned much from this book and look forward to sharing it with my sons."

—*Dr. Iain M. Duguid*
Professor of Old Testament
Westminster Theological Seminary, Philadelphia

THE
MASCULINE
MANDATE

THE
MASCULINE
MANDATE

God's Calling to Men

Richard D. Phillips

 LIGONIER MINISTRIES

The Masculine Mandate: God's Calling to Men
© 2010 by Richard D. Phillips

Published by Ligonier Ministries
421 Ligonier Court, Sanford, FL 32771
Ligonier.org

Printed in Ann Arbor, Michigan
Cushing-Malloy, Inc.
0000421
First edition, ninth paperback printing

ISBN 978-1-56769-684-4 (Paperback)
ISBN 978-1-56769-120-7 (Hardcover)
ISBN 978-1-56769-217-4 (ePub)
ISBN 978-1-56769-452-9 (Kindle)

Cover design: Ryan Harrison
Interior design and typeset: Katherine Lloyd, The DESK

Unless otherwise noted, Scripture quotations are from the ESV® Bible (The Holy Bible, English Standard Version®), copyright © 2001 by Crossway, a publishing ministry of Good News Publishers. Used by permission. All rights reserved.

Scripture references marked NIV are from *The Holy Bible, New International Version*®. NIV®. Copyright © 1973, 1978, 1984 by International Bible Society. Used by permission of Zondervan. All rights reserved.

The Library of Congress has catalogued the hardcover edition as follows:

Phillips, Richard D. (Richard Davis), 1960-
 The masculine mandate : God's calling to men / Richard D. Phillips.
   p. cm.
 Includes indexes.
 ISBN 978-1-56769-120-7
 1. Men (Christian theology) 2. Christian men--Religious life. 3. Christian men--Conduct of life. I. Title.
  BT703.5.P45 2009
  270.081--dc22

                          2009028263

To Sharon,
my greatest help in this world,
and to our sons, Matthew and Jonathan

Contents

Foreword

W hat image comes to your mind when you hear the expression "A man's man"? Is it the picture of an outdoorsman, skilled in hunting and fishing? Might it be the idea of a man capable of building his own house? Is it more along the lines of a tough guy in the mold of John Wayne?

There's certainly nothing wrong with being an outdoorsman, building one's own house, or even, within bounds, being the solid John Wayne type. But is that all there is to being a man? The truth is that the Bible gives us God's picture of a real man, and it doesn't fit any of our stereotypes.

God begins to paint His picture of manhood in Genesis 1, where we read of man's creation in the image of God. He continues to work on His portrait in Genesis 2, which tells us that God planted a garden in Eden and put man there to work it and keep it.

Isn't it interesting that the first thing God says about the role of man is that he is to work? In fact, the necessity and value of work is assumed throughout the Bible and is stated explicitly in a number of Scripture passages. For example, the writer of Ecclesiastes said, "Behold, what I have seen to be good and fitting is to eat and drink and find enjoyment in all the toil with which one toils under the sun the few days of his life that God has given him, for this is his lot" (Eccl. 5:18). Turning to the New Testament, Paul exhorts us to "work heartily, as for the Lord" (Col. 3:23) and warns that "If anyone is not willing to work, let him not eat" (2 Thess. 3:10). Also, we will be working in the new earth.

I find this biblical emphasis on work quite encouraging. Very few of us men fit any of the stereotypes of the "man's man." But we all can fulfill God's mandate to work. In that sense, we can see ourselves in God's picture of a real man.

But there's more to the picture than work. When God put Adam in the garden to work, He gave him Eve as a helper (Gen. 2:18, 21–23). So man is to work and, generally speaking, he is to marry. Of course, there will always be God-ordained exceptions, but God's normal plan is that men are to take wives and "be fruitful and multiply and fill the earth" (Gen. 1:28). Therefore, the humble working man, toiling faithfully at his job, nurturing and shepherding his wife, and seeking to bring up his children in the discipline and instruction of the Lord, conforms to God's picture of a real man. He may indeed be a hunter and fisherman, he may be capable of building his own house, or he may even be a John Wayne hero type. But those abilities and character traits are at best secondary to the basic roles of diligent worker and faithful and caring husband and father.

In this excellent book, Rick Phillips covers these subjects and much more in a thoroughly biblical fashion. All that he says is based solidly on Scripture, so he gives us an accurate picture of what it means to be God's man. The reader will come away reassured that even though he may possess none of the attributes that the world deems essential for a "man's man," nevertheless he can be one of God's men.

This is not an entertaining book, but it is a valuable book. Every Christian man who reads it carefully and seeks to apply it to his own life will profit immensely. A few will see that their lives already generally conform to the biblical principles Rick sets forth, and will thus be encouraged to keep on living as they are now doing. Others will see attitudes and actions in their lives that fall shy of the biblical pattern for men, and they will be instructed and motivated to seek change where appropriate.

By God's grace, this book will help men to hear those blessed words at the ends of their lives: "Well done, good and faithful servant. You have been faithful over a little; I will set you over much. Enter into the joy of your master" (Matt. 25:23).

—Jerry Bridges
Colorado Springs, June 2009

Preface

It is remarkable to me how easily precious things can be lost. An individual can quickly lose precious possessions such as innocence, integrity, or a good reputation. The church can lose precious things, too, and this seems to be happening today. One ideal we may be losing is that of strong, biblical, and confident Christian manhood. Not long ago, we were all told to get in touch with our "feminine side" (as I'll note again later, mine is named Sharon), and this sort of cultural foolishness has resulted in many men misperceiving what it means to be a godly man, a loving husband, a good father, and a faithful friend.

This book is written for Christian men who not only don't want to lose that precious biblical understanding, but who want to live out the calling to true manliness God has given us. We need to be godly men, and the Bible presents a Masculine Mandate for us to follow and fulfill. But do we know what it is? My aim in writing this book is to help men to know and fulfill the Lord's calling as it is presented so clearly to us in God's Word.

Again, I have little doubt that today's problem with true manliness arises in large part from a broader problem in the secular culture. So many young men grow up today without a father—or with a father who is inadequately connected with his sons—that there is bound to be confusion about masculinity. The secular media bombard us all with images and models of womanhood and manhood that are simply bogus. Meanwhile, in growing numbers of evangelical churches, the presence of strong and godly men seems to have receded in the face of a feminized spirituality. In the affluence of our postmodern Western society, men typically no longer engage in the kind of struggle for survival that used to turn boys into men. Yet our families and churches need strong, masculine Christian men as much—or more—than they ever have. So how do we revive or recover our threatened masculinity? The place to start, as always, is in God's Word, with its strong vision and clear teaching on what it means not just to be male but to be a man of God.

The purpose of this book is to provide straight, clear, and pointed teaching on what the Bible says to men as men. I write this, not looking down on today's guy—thankfully, I am neither old enough nor grumpy enough for that yet!—but as a brother in Christ who believes in the Bible and has had reason (both personal and pastoral) to search God's Word for guidance on manhood. This is a journey I have been on for quite a while. What does it mean for me to be the Christian man that I want to be, that my family needs me to be, and that God has made and redeemed me in Christ to be? For me, the journey has involved a blend of renewal and repentance. Things that I thought were manly really aren't, and things that God has called me to do have needed to be done. The result, however, has been both clarity and calling—and what a blessing these are!

My hope and prayer is that other men and churches can be

helped by this tour through the Bible's teaching on manhood, for the Masculine Mandate to which God calls us is intended to bear great fruit for His glory in this fallen world. If we do not seek truth in this matter from God, then something not only precious but essential will be lost from our churches: biblical models of godly masculinity for our boys and for male converts to follow, and the manly leadership God has ordained as intrinsic to the strength and health of His church.

I want to express my thanks to the Session and congregation of Second Presbyterian Church in Greenville, South Carolina, for their devoted support of my ministry of God's Word. What a joy it is to preach the Scriptures to such an eager Christian family! I also thank my many friends at Ligonier Ministries who have partnered with me in every aspect of this book—especially my editors, Greg Bailey and Kevin Meath, who have made terrific contributions. Finally, I thank my faithful and loving wife, Sharon, for her model of godly femininity and the loving support that she so freely gives to me, along with our five children, who cheerfully endure numerous sacrifices so that their parents may serve the Lord. To Him be glory.

Part One

UNDERSTANDING OUR MANDATE

Chapter 1

MAN IN
THE GARDEN

I think it's not a bad idea to begin this book on masculinity by recalling something I read in a sports magazine in a barber shop. Not a hair salon—a barber shop! The article was about the new nonconventional sports, focusing especially on Moto-X freestyle motocross. These are the sports of people who jump motorcycles over buildings or hang from the handlebars while somersaulting their bikes fifty feet in the air. The leading figure in this sport is Brian Deegan, who, it turns out, recently became a Christian.

In 1997, Deegan formed the Metal Mulisha freestyle motocross team. Over the next eight years, Deegan and his friends won numerous races and jumping competitions while establishing their reputation for mayhem, destruction, and violence. Their lifestyle was emblemized by their tattoos and Nazi symbolism, and focused mainly on motorcycles, alcohol, drugs, sex, and fighting.

Three things happened to Deegan that led to a radical change. The first was that his girlfriend became pregnant and insisted on keeping their child. The second was a failed attempt at a high-speed midair backflip in the 2006 X-Games that nearly ended Deegan's life and led to months of physical rehabilitation. The third was his agreement to attend church with his girlfriend. To his surprise, he didn't hate it and, before long, he had come to saving faith in Jesus. As a result, he married his girlfriend and quit drinking and drugs; another result was that he invited his fellow Metal Mulisha bikers to study the Bible with him. One by one, many were born again to faith in Jesus. "He kept telling us how much the Bible changed his life," one recalled. "I felt like I had to listen." Deegan, once the epitome of the angry, foulmouthed insurrectionist, now sits with a Bible open on his lap and tells sports journalists that he wants his daughter to be able to look up to his example as a Christian father.[1]

I have kept up with Deegan from time to time since reading that article. If you check up on this young Christian, you will find that he has plenty of growth in godliness still to do, but what is most important is that he knows it. When asked in one interview about the obvious changes in his lifestyle, Deegan answered with these immortal words: "I had kids and I have to be a role model to represent to my kids. . . . I had to grow up, had to be a man, had to be a father, and so I did it, dude."[2] My guess is that as Deegan grows as a Christian, he will learn more and more that he has not yet "done it, dude." There is plenty of growing up that all Christian men still need to do. But here is the question that comes to my mind: once a Brian Deegan realizes God is calling him to be a man, where can a dude like him find out how?

When it comes to practically every question about God's intentions for men and women, the answer is almost always the same: go back to the garden. When Jesus was asked about marriage (Matt. 19:4–6), He answered from Genesis 2. Likewise, when Paul was discussing the role of women in relation to men (1 Tim. 2:11–14), he found his answers in Genesis 2. The New Testament sees issues of gender and male-female relationships answered in the opening chapters of the Bible: the basic teaching on creation in Genesis 1 and the record of God's specific dealing with the first man and woman in Genesis 2. It is here that we should search for the Bible's most basic teaching on manhood.

MANHOOD: THE WHO, WHERE, WHAT, AND HOW

Just as we will never understand God's rules for marriage and His calling for husbands and wives unless we understand Genesis 2, we likewise will never understand what it means to be a man—single or married—without studying this vitally important chapter. Genesis 2 tells us four essential things about man: *who* man is, *where* man is, *what* man is, and *how* man is to fulfill his calling. This is obviously very important stuff, essential to an accurate understanding of our calling as men.

Who We Are: Spiritual Creatures

Genesis 2:7 tells of God's special formation of man: "then the Lord God formed the man of dust from the ground and

5

breathed into his nostrils the breath of life, and the man became a living creature." This creation of man is unique in two ways.

First, God made no other creature with such hands-on care. To create the animals, God simply spoke, and His declaration was enough. But God formed man from the dust, molding us with fatherly care.

Second, God then breathed into man His own breath—the breath of life eternal. I'm going to come back to man's creation identity in Chapter 4, but for now we should realize that this means God made man to be different. We are not just one more kind of creature among many. Men and women are *spiritual* creatures. Earlier, the Bible says that God made man "in his own image" (Gen. 1:27). Both in our mortal bodies and in our immortal spirits (that breath of life from God) we have been *enabled* to know God and *called* to bear His image in the created world.

God has given us a spiritual nature so that we may bear His image as His worshipers and servants. This is who we are as men.

Where God Put Us: Covenant vs. the Wild at Heart Fallacy

The next verse, Genesis 2:8, tells us important information that is easily overlooked. Once God made this man into something unique—a spiritual creature—where on the great globe of the earth did He put him? After all, there was only one Adam, he could only be in one place, and throughout the process of creation God was clearly being very intentional in His every action. Certainly the placement of man would be equally intentional. The answer is: "the LORD God planted a garden in Eden, in the east, and there he put the man whom he had formed."

The Garden of Eden is described in the Bible as a small corner of the originally created world that God had made rich and beautiful. Adam was put in the garden, along with Eve, with the command to "be fruitful and multiply and fill the earth and subdue it and have dominion" (Gen. 1:28).

How are we to think of this garden? The garden is the place where God relates covenantally to his creature man and where God brings the man into covenantal relationships and obligations. In terms of the Bible's story of man, the garden was originally where all the action was. Adam was to enter into God's work of creation, starting in the garden, which he was to cultivate and work so that God's glory would grow and spread, and the knowledge of God would extend throughout the cosmos. The *where* of man, at least prior to Adam's fall into sin (Gen. 3), is the garden—the God-made realm of covenantal relationships and duties to the glory of the Lord.

At this point, I have the unpleasant duty of correcting some erroneous teaching that has gained prominence in recent years. Since its publication in 2001, the top Christian book on manhood has been John Eldredge's *Wild at Heart*. This book has become practically a cottage industry, complete with supporting videos, workbooks, and even a "Field Manual." In my opinion, *Wild at Heart* gained traction with Christian men in large part because it calls us to stop being sissies, to cease trying to get in touch with our "feminine side" (mine is named Sharon), and instead to embark on an exciting quest to discover our male identity. I can add my hearty "Amen!" to the idea that Christian men should reject a feminized idea of manhood. The problem is that the basic approach to masculinity presented in *Wild at Heart* is almost precisely opposite from what is really taught in the Bible. For this reason, this book has, in my opinion, sown much confusion among men seeking a truly biblical sense of masculinity.

We encounter major errors in *Wild at Heart* right at the beginning, where Eldredge discusses Genesis 2:8: "Eve was created within the lush beauty of Eden's garden. But Adam, if you'll remember, was created *outside* the garden, in the wilderness."[3] Eldredge reasons here that if God "put the man" into the garden, he must have been made outside the garden. While the Bible does not actually say this, it's plausible. But even assuming it's true, what are we to make of it? Eldredge makes an unnecessary and most unhelpful leap of logic, concluding that the "core of a man's heart is undomesticated,"[4] and because we are "wild at heart," our souls must belong in the wilderness and not in the cultivated garden. That is, Eldredge assumes and then teaches as a point of doctrine a view of manhood that Scripture simply does not support.

It's easy to understand how this teaching has appealed to men who labor in office buildings or feel imprisoned by the obligations of marriage, parenthood, and civilized society. But there is one thing Eldredge does not notice. God *put* the man in the garden. The point of *Wild at Heart* is that a man finds his identity outside the garden in wilderness quests. In contrast, the point of Genesis 2:8 is that God has put the man into the garden, into the world of covenantal relationships and duties, in order to gain and act out his God-given identity there. If God intends men to be wild at heart, how strange that he placed man in the garden, where his life would be shaped not by self-centered identity quests but by covenantal bonds and blessings.

What We Are: Lords and Servants

"Be fruitful and multiply and fill the earth," God tells Adam and Eve together (Gen. 1:28). Here we begin to see the *what* of maleness, namely, that Adam was put in the garden to be its lord and servant. Adam was to bring glory to God by devoting himself to bearing God's fruit, starting in the garden and extending outward to all of creation. For this reason, Adam was God's assistant lord, exercising authority over creation: "Subdue it and have dominion over the fish of the sea and over the birds of the heavens and over every living thing that moves on the earth" (Gen. 1:28).

This is the calling of mankind as a whole—men and women together—but of males especially. God placed Adam in a leadership role toward Eve, referring to her as Adam's "helper" (Gen. 2:18, 20). God made the woman for Adam, and it was Adam who named the woman, as he had named all the other creatures, for Adam was the lord of the garden, serving and representing the Lord his God, who is over all. Adam was not to devote himself, therefore, to endless quests for his masculine identity, but he was to be lord and keeper of God's created realm, bringing glory to the Creator as he sought to bear the image of God in servant faithfulness.

How We Obey God: Work and Keep

Genesis 2:7–8 tells us *who* man is, a spiritual creature made so as to know and glorify God; *where* man is, placed by God in the heart of the garden that God made; and *what* man is, the lord and servant of God's created glory. Finally, by going forward a handful of verses to Genesis 2:15, we learn *how* man is to fulfill his calling: "The LORD God took the man and put him in the garden of Eden to work it and keep it."

To work it and keep it: here is the *how* of biblical masculinity, the mandate of Scripture for males. It is my mandate in this book, therefore, to seek to specify, clarify, elaborate, and apply these two verbs to the glorious, God-given, lifelong project of masculine living:

Work. To work is to labor to make things grow. In subsequent chapters I will discuss work in terms of nurturing, cultivating, tending, building up, guiding, and ruling.

Keep. To keep is to protect and to sustain progress already achieved. Later I will speak of it as guarding, keeping safe, watching over, caring for, and maintaining.

Conceptually there is some overlap between these terms, and in practice acts of working and keeping frequently intermingle. It seems that God was using these two complementary terms to indicate the package of attitudes and behaviors that would constitute manhood as He intended it to function. It is helpful, therefore, to see the Genesis 2:15 "work" and "keep" roles as separate but related. Two words that serve as good summaries of both terms are *service* and *leadership*, modern words that relate closely to the biblical words *servant* and *lord*.

Based on the teaching of Genesis 2, men are to enter into the world God has made as the men He has made us to be—lords and servants under God's authority—that we might fulfill our mandate: to work and to keep.

THE ADVENTURE BEGINS

Let me end this chapter by going back to Brian Deegan. The last thing this brother needs to be told—newly married, with his little baby on his lap, and through his God-given talent holding a position of influence among his generation—is that God wants him to look on life as a series of ego-adventures in the wilderness so that he might find his masculine self. That is precisely what Deegan was doing *prior* to becoming a Christian. Indeed, this is what modern and postmodern masculinity has been all about—men behaving like little boys forever, serving themselves in the name of self-discovery. (Can we imagine someone like Ronald Reagan or Winston Churchill talking about going on a quest to find his masculine self? They were too busy changing the world.)

God has something far more exciting for Brian Deegan, for you, and for me. For it is in obedience to Scripture that the adventure of a man's life truly begins. God calls us to bear

His image in the real world, in this garden that has become corrupted by sin but is being redeemed by the power of God's grace in Christ. He calls us to do this by being leaders and servants in the ultimate cause of displaying God's glory and bearing the fruit of God's love in real relationships. That is the Masculine Mandate: to be spiritual men placed in real-world, God-defined relationships, as lords and servants under God, to bear God's fruit by serving and leading.

If you think this sounds boring and that you might prefer to pursue wilderness living on a quest to gratify your own ego, let me encourage you to stick around through Chapter 5 as we mine more deeply the teaching of Genesis 2. Then, if the case I will try to make doesn't seem convincing, if you still want to drop out and live the rest of your life for your own glory, go right ahead. But the rest of us are going to press on to apply our masculine calling in all of the covenant relationships of life: marriage, fatherhood, friendship, and church. As we do this, we will find that pursuing God's simple mandate for men provides clarity and meaning for our lives—and, yes, adventure too. To live for God's glory, fulfilling our calling "to work and to keep" with respect to those people and pursuits placed in our care—this is what it means as men, created for God and placed in the world, to bear fruit in His name.

I hope you join us.

Questions for Reflection and Discussion

- How is it different to find your masculine identity in the Bible rather than in a life of self-serving quests?

Why is God's Word a safer guide than our own sub-jective spiritual experience?

- Genesis 2 says that a man's identity includes servant lordship on God's behalf. What responsibilities has God given you and what authority has He placed into your hands? How should you act so that God is pleased and His name is praised? Are there any future responsibilities for which you should be pre-paring now? How might you do that?

- Why does God want our masculine identity to be forged in the garden rather than out in the wilder-ness? Why is it important that men find their calling in God-given relationships?

Chapter 2

THE MASCULINE MANDATE

I come from a cavalry family, as in horse soldiers. My great-grandfather was a cavalry scout in the frontier West. My grandfather commanded the Army's last horse cavalry regiment (in 1938, believe it or not). At that point, our family switched from horses to tanks, and both my father and I served as tank officers. Suffice it to say that I possess a fair amount of cavalry paraphernalia. In fact, I am writing this chapter at a desk beneath a print of a horse cavalryman firing from his saddle.

Of all the great cavalry movies, none holds a dearer place in my heart than John Wayne's classic *She Wore a Yellow Ribbon*. Portraying Captain Nathan Briddles, a grizzled Civil War veteran who is facing the end of his career, the Duke is a walking cornucopia of manliness. When I was a young armored cav officer, I not only watched this movie roughly a thousand times but absorbed much of its ethos. Anyone who has seen this movie can tell you that Captain Briddles' approach to manliness can be summed up in two words: *Never apologize!* Over and over again, he grills his hapless lieutenants, always with the same emphasis: "Never apologize, Mister!" I am afraid that I took this counsel a bit too much to heart, with the result that my early twenties were a little more obnoxious than they needed to be.

When I became a Christian, however, I learned that not every manly saying in John Wayne movies should be adopted. "Never apologize" may sound great in theory, but in practice it can combine with a man's sin nature to make him overbearing and arrogant. As I became more familiar with Scripture, I learned about two different words that do a far better job of summarizing how a man should live. These are the two words you read about in Chapter 1, words we will revisit throughout this book: "work" and "keep."

Taken together, these two words serve as a summary of the Bible's mandate for masculine behavior. Men are called to be men, fulfilling our calling before God in this world: "The Lord God took the man and put him in the garden of Eden to work it and keep it" (Gen. 2:15). Our calling in life really is this simple (although not therefore easy): We are to devote ourselves to working/building and keeping/protecting everything placed into our charge.

What exactly do these two words signify? Let's take a few moments to look more closely.

WORK: TO CULTIVATE AS A GARDENER

First, let's consider *avad*, the Hebrew term translated in Genesis 2:15 as "work." This is an extremely common word in the Old

Testament, and can appear in a verb or noun form. As a verb, it most often means "work," "serve," "labor," "cultivate," or "perform acts of worship." As a noun, it usually indicates "servant," "officer," or "worshiper." Because the context for Genesis 2 is the Garden of Eden, we should first consider how *avad* applies in an agricultural sense. Adam was called by God to till and cultivate the garden so it would grow and bear an abundance of fruit. Thus, the command to "work" links up with the earlier mandate to "be fruitful . . . and fill the earth" (Gen. 1:28).

What does a gardener do to make his garden grow? He tends the garden; he *works* it. He plants seeds and prunes branches. He digs and fertilizes. His labor makes living things strong, beautiful, and lush. As he works, he is able to stand back and see that he has accomplished good things. There are rows of tall trees, rich fields of wheat, bountiful vineyards, and colorful beds of flowers.

My favorite summer job in college was working for a landscaper. Every day we would drive out to a job site—often someone's home—to plant trees, build garden walls, and put in rows of bushes. It was hard but satisfying work. The thing I liked best was looking in the mirror as we drove away to see that we had accomplished something good and growing.

According to the Bible, this kind of work describes one of the two main planks in a man's calling. Not that men are all literally to work as gardeners. Rather, we are called to "work" whatever "field" God has given us. Men are to be planters, builders, and growers. A man's working life is to be spent accomplishing things, usually as part of a company or other grouping of people. We are to invest our time, our energies, our ideas, and our passions in bringing good things into being. A faithful man, then, is one who has devoted himself to cultivating, building, and growing.

Take a Christian man's professional life, for example. I'm going to address this in more detail in the next chapter, but for now let's observe that our calling to work means investing ourselves in accomplishing things of value. Men should be using their gifts, talents, and experiences to succeed in worthwhile causes that (if they are married) provide for their families. This can be anything that accomplishes good. A man can make eyeglasses, do scientific research, or manage a store; the examples are almost endless. But in each case, our mandate to work means we should be devoting ourselves to building good things and accomplishing worthwhile results. There is nothing wrong with a man working simply to earn a wage, but Christians rightly want their labors to yield more than money for themselves and their families. Christian men should also desire to cultivate something worthwhile for the glory of God and the well-being of their fellow men.

Of course, our "garden" includes not merely things but people. Several chapters in this book focus on relationships, but for now let us simply recognize that men's calling to cultivate means we are to be involved in the hearts of people placed under our care—people who work for us, people we teach and mentor, and most especially our wives and children. A man's fingers should be accustomed to working in the soil of the human heart—the hearts of those he serves and loves—that he

18

might accomplish some of the most valuable and important work of this life.

This biblical mandate to work—here with the emphasis on cultivating and tending—explodes a great misconception regarding gender roles. We have been taught that women are the main nurturers, while men are to be "strong and silent." But the Bible calls men to be cultivators, and that includes a significant emphasis on tending the hearts of those given into our charge.

A husband is called to nurture his wife emotionally and spiritually. This is not a side show to his calling as a husband but is fundamental and central to his masculine calling in marriage. Likewise, a father is called to be intentional about plowing up and nurturing the hearts of his children. Any counselor who has dealt with childhood issues can tell you that few things are more injurious to a child than emotional distance from his or her father. There is a reason why so many people are hung up over their relationship with their fathers: God has given the primary calling of emotional and spiritual nurture to men, and many of us fail to do it well.

It is the male arm around the shoulder or pat on the back that God allows to have the quickest access to the heart of a child or employee. Men who are seeking to live out the Masculine Mandate will be nurturers.

KEEP: TO PROTECT AS A SWORD-BEARER

The other half of the Masculine Mandate is found in the word *keep*. Here, the basic meaning is to "guard" or "protect." This is captured in another common Hebrew word, *shamar*, which is translated by such English terms as "watch," "guard," "protect," "take under custody," or "exercise care." The word is used of soldiers, shepherds, priests, custodians, and government officials. I especially love the way God uses this word regarding Himself. The Lord frequently states that He guards and keeps those who trust in Him. In fact, *shamar* is the idea behind the powerful biblical image of the Lord as a tower or strong fortress.

Take, for instance, the great words of Psalm 121, which begins: "I lift up my eyes to the hills. From where does my help come? My help comes from the LORD, who made heaven and earth" (vv. 1–2). As we continue the psalm, we see that most of the help God gives us comes in the form of "keeping," the very same word used of Adam's calling in Genesis 2:15. The psalm says, "He will not let your foot be moved; he who keeps you will not slumber" (Ps. 121:3). This says that God is watching over His people so that we will not fall down. "Behold, he who keeps Israel will neither slumber nor sleep" (Ps. 121:4). The Lord is always on the job, guarding His people. The psalm concludes, "The LORD will keep you from all evil; he will keep your life. The LORD will keep your going out and your coming in from this time forth and forevermore" (Ps. 121:7–8). God watches over believers at all times, to protect us from harm and especially to preserve our immortal souls for Himself. What a wonderful description of God's keeping ministry. His calling to Christian men is similar: we are to watch over and keep safe all that the Lord has put under our care.

This calling to *keep* rounds out the Masculine Mandate of the Bible. A man is not only to wield the plow but also to bear the sword. Being God's deputy lord in the garden, Adam was not only to make it fruitful but also to keep it safe. Likewise, our basic mandate as Christian men is to cultivate, build, and grow (both things and people), but also to stand guard so that people and things are kept safe—so that the fruit of past cultivating and nurturing is preserved.

To be a man is to stand up and be counted when there is danger or other evil. God does not desire for men to stand by idly and allow harm, or permit wickedness to exert itself. Rather, we are called to keep others safe within all the covenant relationships we enter. In our families, our presence is to make our wives and children feel secure and at ease. At church, we are to stand for truth and godliness against the encroachment of worldliness and error. In society, we are to take our places as men who stand up against evil and who defend the nation from threat of danger.

WHAT GREATNESS LOOKS LIKE

The rest of this book will apply this Masculine Mandate to the various arenas of manly life and service: work, home, and the local church. "The Lord God took the man and put him in the garden of Eden to work it and keep it" (Gen. 2:15), and He is still calling on men to cause good things to grow and to keep precious things safe. If we reflect a moment, these are the commitments we tend to admire in great men, and this should not surprise us. Truly great men are servants who give themselves to a worthy cause and leaders who stand for what is right. Come to think of it, this is what we admired in all those John Wayne movies. Take away the dumb saying, "Never apologize," from *She Wore a Yellow Ribbon,* and we see that practically everything Captain Briddles did fell into the categories of building up or keeping safe.

If we want to be the men God is calling us to be—men who are rightly admired and respected by those we love, men who faithfully fulfill our duty before God—then we will make as our motto and watchword the Masculine Mandate that we as men have received from God: We will *work* and *keep.*

Questions for Reflection and Discussion

- The author expresses concern that men have been taught to be "strong and silent." What is wrong with a man being emotionally distant?

- How have you benefited from another man's heart-cultivating ministry to you? How have you felt the lack of it? What are the relationships in which the Lord would challenge you to be more involved to nurture and cultivate growth?

- Genesis 2:15 shows that men are to be guardian-protectors. What are the threats to people or things under your care? How should you be thinking about your calling to keep them safe?

- The author states that the Masculine Mandate is "simple, but not easy." Is this a simple set of ideas? If so, does that make them unimportant? Why is it not easy to fulfill this mandate, if the ideas are simple? What changes are needed in your life that you might better embrace the calling God gave to men in the garden?

Chapter 3

MAN'S SACRED CALLING TO WORK

Nobody respects a man who doesn't work. It's just as simple as that. It's OK for a man to be dumb or ugly or even a little unpleasant, so long as he works hard. But nothing is worse than a guy who won't work.

Consider the scorn the apostle Paul heaps upon a lazy man: "If anyone is not willing to work, let him not eat" (2 Thess. 3:10). Christianity does not say, "Well, if he won't work, we'll just give him what he needs." No, Paul says, "Let him starve until he starts working." Why is this? Because men are made by God to work. Men have a duty to work. Men like to work and they feel really good when they work hard. The life of a man is a life of work. This is good and it pleases God.

WORK IN THE HERE AND NOW

I am not trying to romanticize work. I realize that at times many men tolerate, dislike, or even hate their jobs. But underlying so much of the frustration with unsatisfying labor is the knowledge, deep in a man's heart, that work is supposed to be meaningful and enjoyable.

The guys who collect garbage in my neighborhood almost always look like they enjoy their work. Usually operating in teams of three, these men are a well-oiled machine. One drives the truck with skill and gusto, while the other two hustle like athletes to grab the streetside cans and empty them into the crusher, hopping a ride on the back of the truck when necessary. In my limited interactions with these men, they are pleasant and intently focused on their work. Theirs might not be a position many of us would aspire to, it can't be particularly pleasant, and I don't imagine many of them do it for their entire careers, but it is honest, honorable labor, and from all appearances they find it satisfying. To me, this speaks volumes about the inherent value of work.

Work, Identity, and the Effect of Sin

Probably every man has tasted at some time the deep satisfaction of a job well done. Why does labor have this inherent value? *Because we were made for it.* God placed Adam in the garden and put him to work. Therefore, because God is good and has chosen to be glorified through our labor, we are able to enjoy work and find a significant part of our identity in it. In fact, as we keep work in proper balance, retaining our primary identity in Christ, God wants us to invest significant passion in our work and find true meaning in it.

At various times, all of us struggle with the temptations of worldly glory, self-serving power, or the sinful pleasures that can be associated with work. Sometimes we may find that far too much of our identity has become wrapped up in who we are professionally. Of course, none of this is work's fault. It all grows out of our sinful hearts and our tragic ability to stain anything we touch with idolatry and selfishness. Yet our sinfulness does not alter the fact that work is a man's sacred calling, received from the very hand of God himself.

In fact, although the introduction of sin into the garden changed the *nature* of work, God's calling for man to work is entirely holy and good. Bruce Waltke rightly says, "Work is a gift of God, not a punishment for sin. Even before the fall humanity [had] duties to perform."[5] It was after God told Adam to be fruitful—by means of his work—that God declared that creation was "very good" (Gen. 1:31).

After Adam's fall, it remained good for man to work. But due to God's curse on the earth because of human sin, it became necessary for man not merely to work, but to work *hard*:

> "Cursed is the ground because of you; in pain you shall eat of it all the days of your life; thorns and thistles it shall bring forth for you; and you shall eat the plants of the field. By the sweat of your face you shall eat bread, till you return to the ground, for out of it you were taken; for you are dust, and to dust you shall return." (Gen. 3:17–19)

In our fallen world, shadowed by the curse of death and futility, we either work hard or our families suffer. According to the book of Proverbs, industry is an essential characteristic that men should cultivate: "A slack hand causes poverty, but the hand of the diligent makes rich" (Prov. 10:4); "Whoever is slothful will not roast his game, but the diligent man will get precious wealth" (Prov. 12:27). Yet I sometimes hear pastors or Christian psychologists tell men they should never be late for dinner or have to travel away from home for work. I disagree. It's true that men should not pursue their work so single-mindedly that family duties are excluded or consistently compromised. But in our fallen world, men have an obligation to hustle and give their all in the workplace—and this may involve some late nights and business trips. Of all men, Christians should work especially hard, giving *more* than an honest day's work for a day's wage.

In thinking about how the need to work is hardwired into men's souls, and the pleasure we can derive from work, I find it interesting that even many of the things we designate as hobbies are really forms of work. Some men like to relax through woodworking, which is, of course, a matter of *working* with wood. Other men like to work in the garden or restore cars. Some men like to go fishing, which is a kind of work, and others like climbing mountains, which seems like a lot of work. My love for following baseball involves detailed mathematics, which makes the pastime all that much more fun for me. Even in our leisure, we see that men are made for work.

Daily Echoes of Genesis 2

Have you noticed that, almost every time, the second subject that comes up when two men meet involves work? I sit next to a man on an airplane, and what does he ask? "What's your name?" I answer, "I'm Rick Phillips." The next question is amazingly consistent: "What do you do?" How we answer tells people what to think of us.

There are a number of ways I can answer the question. I can say, "I'm an author," in which case the man thinks I'm an interesting person with lots of insight. Or I can say, "I'm an educator." Then he thinks I'm a person with specialized knowledge, and he questions me further to find out what that area of knowledge is. If I say, "I'm a preacher," he starts looking out the window, afraid I'm going to hassle him about his sins. (Usually, the answer I choose to give depends on whether I am interested in talking or not.) The point is that the answer to "What do you do?" tells people most of what they want to know about a man.

In a world in which God has called men to work, this should not be surprising. Do you see the theological tie-back here? In this mundane example, we catch a glimmer of the profundity of Scripture, the kind of glimmer we notice all the time if we're paying attention. The simple who-is-this-guy conversations we have with strangers are not random events. They sprout from the theology of work and calling rooted in the garden and recorded in Genesis 2.

WORK IN HEAVEN

So central is work to a man's calling that, along with worship, Christians will be working even in heaven. We see this in Jesus' parable of the ten minas.

The parable says that a lord went away, entrusting a large sum of money to his servants. Ten of them each received a mina, worth about six months' wages. When the lord returned, he demanded an accounting. (This is yet another passage in which we see men's calling to work.) One of his servants presented a profit of ten more minas, to which the Lord replied, "Well done, good servant! Because you have been faithful in a very little, you shall have authority over ten cities" (Luke 19:17). Another servant had earned five minas, and received authority over five cities (Luke 19:18–19). Jesus taught this to instruct us about His own return and the reward that will be given to His faithful servants. What is our reward? Not a vacation but a promotion! Our reward is the capacity for increased work alongside our Lord in heaven.

We see the same thing in Matthew's parable of the talents. One of the servants invested his five talents and made five more. Jesus said to him, "Well done, good and faithful servant. You have been faithful over a little; I will set you over much. Enter into the joy of your master" (Matt. 25:21). Notice, again, that the reward for faithful service is the opportunity for more glorious, eternal labor with Jesus in the new heaven and new earth after Jesus returns and the cosmos are reborn (see Matt. 19:28; Rom. 8:19–23). Jesus calls this entering "into the joy of your master," which at least includes the joy of His heavenly work. This is the blessing to which we are saved. I do not have any idea what it will be like to work in heaven, but I am certain that it will be more satisfying than the most enjoyable recreation I have ever experienced here on earth.

THE RIGHT WORK FOR YOU HERE

Does this mean that all work is equal? Of course not. Worldly people assess the value of a job by the amount of money it pays or the prestige it offers. Surely, Christians will think differently. Our concerns should be:

- Does this work glorify God?

- Does it benefit my fellow man?

- Do I consider myself called to this work, or can I at least do it well and find enjoyment in that?

- Does it provide for material needs?

- Does it permit me to lead a godly and balanced life?

Glorify God

The Lord made us and redeemed us that we might bear His image and serve the cause of His glory. This is why we exist. Because our work is so central to who we are, we must ask whether it opposes this purpose by bringing us into associations or activities that are sinful. Do my job requirements cause me to compromise truly biblical standards of behavior? A negative example would be a sales job that involves deception or a management position that requires employee abuse. A good question is, "Would I be embarrassed for my pastor to visit my workplace?"

The Bible says, "You shall love the LORD your God with all your heart and with all your soul and with all your might"

(Deut. 6:5). So we should ask, "Does my work honor God through integrity and decency?"

Serve Others

Christians also should seek to earn their living by making or doing something that benefits other people. To the Old Testament command to love God, Jesus added, "You shall love your neighbor as yourself" (Matt. 22:39). With this in mind, I do not see how Christians can make their living doing work that provides no real benefit to other people. Modern-day snake-oil salesmen, hawking products they know are either worthless or vastly overpriced, are one example. Another would be a day-trader on the stock market who devotes all his energies to buying and selling his own holdings for personal gain with no intention of using the profits to help others. (This is very different from stock brokers, who use their expertise to manage other peoples' money skillfully.)

There are so many ways we can use our gifts and abilities to benefit others. Surely, as Christians, we can find something to do that will benefit other people while honoring God, even if in the end we make a smaller income. As Jesus bluntly put it: "You cannot serve God and money" (Matt. 6:24).

Calling and Enjoyment

The apostles were specially called by Jesus to serve him, and they knew it. Paul described himself this way: "Paul, a servant of Christ Jesus, called to be an apostle, set apart for the gospel of God" (Rom. 1:1; see also Acts 9:15). Ministers of the gospel should have this sense of special calling to their work. Pastors and missionaries should find in their work a sense of divine appointment—drawn from both inward motivation and spiritual equipping—that is confirmed by the church.

People in other professions can certainly feel a similar sense of being "right" for a specific position or type of career. This is often true of those who serve others in very direct ways—doctors and nurses, firefighters, and police officers, for example. Yet this pronounced sense of call is obviously not universal. So if, as a Christian, your non-ministerial job or career does not seem to come with a tangible "seal of approval," it is not necessarily cause for concern. For you the question may simply be, "When I do this job well, is it satisfying?" A positive answer to that question is a good indication that what you do meets the mandate of Genesis 2.

Material Needs

If you find yourself in a job in which you are consistently unable to satisfy basic material needs—for yourself as a single man or as head of your household—with enough left over to save some and tithe to your church, you need to ask yourself two questions. First, *Am I striving for a lifestyle that is unrealistic in light of my income-producing potential?* If you are not overreaching in this area and not giving in to the powerful and often deluding temptations of materialism, then the second question becomes very significant. *Why am I so obviously underemployed, and what do I need to do about it?*

Godly and Balanced Life

If some men are underemployed, others are what might be called overemployed. These are men who find themselves so wrapped up in their jobs that their lives are regularly out of balance. As I said earlier, we should all expect from time to time to have to work long hours or take some business trips. But God never expects us to go for extended periods so consumed by work that we are forced to neglect family, friends, church life, or regular time with God.

SEASONS OF WORK

Obviously, what constitutes the right job or career for a man can change over time. My own work history may provide a helpful illustration.

The summer before my freshman year in college, my family moved to Detroit, Michigan, where the American automobile industry had already begun to show signs of decay. Along with my older brother, I got a job working in a plastics factory that made car parts. It was honest work, making a small but real contribution to the world. However, it was miserable work; the foremen treated us like dirt because we were "college boys." Indeed, it was slave labor. Paul says that those who are stuck in slavery (or in a job like we had) should be content with God's provision. "But if you can gain your freedom," he adds, "avail yourself of the opportunity" (1 Cor. 7:21). Well, as soon as another job came available, my brother and I quit the factory, vowing never to take such a job again.

During the rest of my college years, my summer job was

landscaping. This was manual labor that paid only a decent wage. But I liked working outdoors, enjoyed the camaraderie of the work crews, took satisfaction in what we accomplished, and had only moderate financial needs anyway. Nonetheless, my experience in the manual-labor workforce did sharpen my enthusiasm for my studies. I knew I wanted to find a career that would engage my mind and passions at least as much as it did my legs and arms.

It is not surprising that after graduation from college, I was commissioned into the United States Army. My father and grandfather had been career officers and I had attended college on an ROTC scholarship. My early twenties were spent commanding tank and reconnaissance units that were almost constantly deployed or "in the field" on training missions. These were great days for me, in which my character and leadership were challenged and honed.

By my mid-twenties, I started asking myself whether the Army was really the career I wanted or whether I had just followed naturally in my father's footsteps. The latter was certainly true, but I decided that I would commit myself to my military career. I remember thinking that I would soon like to find a wife and settle down. The problem was that I was still deployed almost all the time. Now commanding larger units or holding more significant staff positions, I was hardly in a position to "settle down."

The opportunity came when the Army sent me to graduate school so that I could teach at West Point. During those two school years, something more important happened to me. I was converted to faith in Christ. I also met my future wife and became engaged. Yet my career path was unchanged. It was only during the years that followed, as God rather forcefully persuaded me that He was calling me to leave the Army and serve Him in the vocational ministry, that I took the frightening step of quitting my career and offering myself for full-time ministry.

The kind of progression I experienced is common for many men. We start out at the bottom, and the difficulty and low rewards of more-menial work motivate us to work hard in school and prepare ourselves for careers that are more rewarding. We try to enter fields in which we have an interest, in which the work will be enjoyable, and in which we can provide for our wives and families. Sometimes the Lord intervenes and redirects us, in which case we need to seek prayerfully to follow His lead.

WORKING TO PLEASE THE LORD

Eric Liddell was a Scottish Christian runner who refused to compete in the 1924 Olympics on the Lord's Day. In *Chariots of Fire*, the movie that chronicles Liddell's bold stand at those Olympic Games, Liddell is depicted sharing with his sister, "When I run, I feel God's pleasure." When this line is quoted among Christians, the perceived pleasure of God is usually presented as a kind of litmus test or affirmation for whether or not we are doing God's will. That's fine as far as it goes, but let us recognize that this test places the focus almost exclusively on the human side. "When I run, I feel. . . ." But the most important part of that statement is the last two words: ". . . God's pleasure." In doing what he was born to do in a way that honored God, the most important thing was not that Liddell *felt* God's pleasure but that he *brought* God pleasure; he pleased God. Likewise, Christian men should use their God-given abilities to the uttermost, seeking to give God pleasure through the labors we offer up to Him.

In all our work as Christian men, whatever season we may be in and wherever we happen to find ourselves on the ladder of our chosen pursuit, the best way for us to honor God in our work is to offer up everything we do directly to the Lord Himself. In all things, our goal should be to please Him. This is what Paul urges: "whatever you do, in word or deed, do everything in the name of the Lord Jesus, giving thanks to God the Father through him" (Col. 3:17).

Because nearly all of us do our work in association with other people, in a practical sense, almost everything we do, we do for others. Those who are on the lower rungs of the ladder are called to serve those above them in ways that please God. Those on the higher rungs are called to lead those below them in ways that please God. Clients have godly obligations to vendors just as vendors do to clients. We do our work *for men* in a manner that will be pleasing *to God.* This involves working with biblical motivations and an attitude of holiness, diligently pursuing excellence, and all the while seeking to love others as we love ourselves.

Serving Those over Us

A Christian worker in a twenty-first-century setting is called to follow Paul's instructions to the Christian servants of ancient Colossae:

Obey in everything those who are your earthly masters, not by way of eye-service, as people-pleasers, but with sincerity of heart, fearing the Lord. Whatever you do, work heartily, as for the Lord and not for men, knowing that from the Lord you will receive the inheritance as your reward. You are serving the Lord Christ. (Col. 3:22–24)

Because school is itself a kind of work, I will use an example from my West Point days to illustrate this. I once had a cadet in my class who was a devoted Christian and a leader in student Bible studies. After he failed an exam, I called him in to discuss the grade. Knowing I was a Christian, he said that I would "understand" that his Bible studies had been more important than studying for the test he had flunked. In fact, I did not understand.

At one level, this cadet was demonstrating a poor grasp of theology. But at the same time, by appealing to our shared faith in an effort to excuse his laziness and wrong priorities, he was being a people-pleaser. After demanding that he stand at attention while I reprimanded him, I informed him that he was disgracing the Lord by failing to uphold his duties as a student. Whether student or employee, we do not honor the Lord if we neglect the work obligations that we have accepted and which others are counting on us to perform.

Leading Those under Us

A preacher should prepare and deliver his sermons for the benefit of the congregation—it is not pleasing to God for a man to preach as if no one is there. But he must preach in a way that first and foremost will be pleasing to the Lord, seeking His approval by being a faithful minister of His Word, *before* considering whether the congregation will like it or not.

Similarly, the first obligation of an employer or manager is not to set policies and pursue goals that focus primarily on making employees as happy and secure as possible. At the same time, he must recognize that God desires for his employees to serve in ways that are meaningful, productive, profitable, and suitable to their gifts and talents. This has numerous implications for the hiring, training, positioning, and rewarding of employees.

Loving Others in Daily Interactions

Doing all things unto the Lord will radically affect the way we treat others in the basic interactions of daily life. Jesus taught that in the final judgment, He will praise His people for the least of the mercies they showed to others in His name:

> "I was hungry and you gave me food, I was thirsty and you gave me drink, I was a stranger and you welcomed me, I was naked and you clothed me, I was sick and you visited me, I was in prison and you came to me." Then the righteous will answer him, saying, "Lord, when did we see you hungry and feed you, or thirsty and give you drink? And when did we see you a stranger and welcome you, or naked and clothe you? And when did we see you sick or in prison and visit you?" And the King will answer them,

"Truly, I say to you, as you did it to one of the least of these my brothers, you did it to me." (Matt. 25:35–40)

Christians who labor unto the Lord remember that God cares about how we treat other people. Because we remember, we make it our own pleasure to glorify Him through sincerity, integrity, kindness, and love. Jesus reminds us that when we stand before Him, the great issue of our lives will not be what achievements we compiled, what honors we won, or what riches we amassed, but how humbly we glorified God and served our fellow man day to day.

AN AUDIENCE OF ONE

I have been helped by an illustration that I often remember and meditate on. The story is that of an accomplished young pianist making his concert debut at Carnegie Hall. His playing was magnificent and after he departed from the stage the audience erupted in cheers. The kindly stage manager urged the young virtuoso to go out for his encore. But the young man refused. The older man replied: "Look out through the curtains. They love you! Go take an encore!" The pianist answered: "Do you see the one old man in the balcony on the left?" The stage manager peered out and answered that he did see him. "That man is seated. I will not give an encore until he stands and cheers." Exasperated, the stage manager said, "Only one man is not standing, and you will not take an encore?" At this, the pianist replied: "You see, that old man is my piano teacher. Only when he stands will I go take an encore."

This story reminds me that we are not to live for the praise of the world, but before an audience of One. If God is pleased with our work, though the whole world oppose us, we can be satisfied. By contrast, if the world is cheering and showering us with rewards, yet God is displeased, then we should rightly reconsider our choices. The young pianist was not playing merely for his teacher; he offered his labor for the blessing of all the people present. The point, rather, is that he understood that the true praise and reward that he ought most to desire was that of his master. So it is for a man of God.

The good news is that as God's "dearly beloved children" (Eph. 5:1) who have been accepted into His favor through the grace of Jesus Christ, we do not live and work before a harsh and difficult God. The illustration should not give us the impression that it is impossible to please our God and Father, even if everyone else loves what we are doing. Rather, it says that we must ultimately measure success according to God's standards, given in His Word. Our labor should be that of faith, offered up for the glory of God and the well-being of our neighbor.

We can be sure that as we serve God faithfully and with a sincere heart, offering up to Him the work that He has given to us and trusting in the blood of Christ to cleanse us from all our sins and faults, our work will receive the Lord's accolades. Whatever crowns He should be pleased to place on our heads, we will be pleased to lay them back at His feet. The Lord is our audience of One, and we serve our fellow man for the sake of God's praise and His pleasure in us.

Questions for Reflection and Discussion

- Do you find that people link your identity to your work? What does your job (or your schooling to prepare for a future job) say about you?

- The author points out that as a result of the fall, a man's work is difficult and demanding. How do you experience this? What frustrations do you face in your working life? How do you manage tensions between the home and workplace so that you can be faithful in both places?

- The author states that men were made for work. Do you find that you enjoy working? Does the biblical material presented here challenge you to reconsider your attitude toward work?

- If you are still in school, how are you preparing now for your future occupation? What specific things might you pray to the Lord about with respect to embracing a man's calling to work?

- How do you feel about your job? Does the material presented here about assessing one's work help you to think about your career? Do you think that what you do honors God and serves others? Would you be willing for your pastor to visit your work site? What changes might you make at your job that would make your service more pleasing to God? Is there a conflict between your boss's expectations and the Lord's expectations for your work? How do you handle any tension between the two?

Chapter 4

MAN AS THE IMAGE OF GOD

I t's time for a trick question: Why are men forbidden from making images that represent God? Because the Lord has commanded man not to *make* an image of God, but to *be* the image of God. We see this in practically the Bible's first teaching about mankind: "God said, 'Let us make man in our image, after our likeness.' . . . So God created man in his own image, in the image of God he created him; male and female he created them" (Gen. 1:26–27).

What does it mean for man to bear God's image? It means that in all this wide creation, with mountains tall to show God's grandeur and rolling oceans to bear witness to His power, with plumed birds to reveal God's artisanship and roaring beasts to display His majesty, God placed mankind on the earth so that God would be specially known amid His creation. This is why, when the Westminster Shorter Catechism poses its first question, "What is the chief end of man?" it answers that "Man's chief end is to glorify God, and to enjoy him for ever." That is, man is to glorify God and delight forever in the knowledge of Him.

"Bear my image," God said, in effect, to Adam and Eve. While the image of God in our race has been marred and damaged by sin, it remains man's calling to bear that image in this world. Today, all men carry that image in some measure—but by grace, Christians carry it in greater measure and are called to spend their lives increasing that measure. This is because, while fallen Adam was still in the garden, a Messiah was promised. The purpose of that Messiah, which He fulfilled perfectly, was to purchase men by His own blood that they might glorify God with their lives, and then—as the catechism says—enjoy Him forever. Therefore, we Christians, purchased by that blood, are called and enabled to bear God's image to a degree that would otherwise be impossible for us. This is why Jesus our Messiah urges us, saying, "Let your light shine before others, so that they may see your good works and give glory to your Father who is in heaven" (Matt. 5:16). As Christian men redeemed from sin, we have been given a high calling indeed.

It may be true that unbelieving men spend their lives trying to "find themselves" and display their own success before the world. But men who have been redeemed from sin through Jesus Christ have been freed from the bondage of self to live for the glory of God in all things. Through the way we live, we want others—our friends, our family members, our co-workers—to see something of the truth and grace of God in Christ, with the aim that they will be encouraged to seek Him for their own salvation. This is the chief end of our lives and our fondest desire: that others would see something of the glory of God—His mercy, His faithfulness, His power, His grace—in us.

BEARING GOD'S IMAGE

In what ways was mankind specially made "in God's image"? By what means are we able to display Him to the world? I would like to touch briefly on three areas in particular.

We Were Created Rational and Spiritual

The traditional answer has been to point to man's dual nature as a creature capable of both rational and spiritual activity. Man alone is able to worship God (spiritual) and has reasoning ability (rational) that far exceeds that of all other species, however impressive their abilities may be. The combination of these two natures distinguishes us from the animals. This is certainly part of what it means for man to bear God's glory. Yet it is not the entire picture.

We Were Granted Dominion over Creation

Another factor is man's dominion over creation, as granted by God. Sandwiched between the two verses that show man to be made in God's image (Gen. 1:26–27) is this mandate to human lordship: "And let them have dominion over the fish of the sea and over the birds of the heavens and over the livestock and over all the earth and over every creeping thing that creeps on the earth" (Gen. 1:26).

This verse indicates that, as bearers of God's image, men and women are to rule over the earth so as to make it fruitful. As Jesus taught us, we should pray, "Thy kingdom come, thy will be done, on earth as it is in heaven" (Matt. 6:10), and to some extent we are to be agents of God's heavenly will—His dominion—on earth. In this sense, we may say that man represents God by exercising His authority over all living things. Man was made as God's regent-ruler over creation. We were designed to bear God's image in the world by implementing God's will.

We Are a Reflection of Original Righteousness

Furthermore, man's creation in God's image reflects Adam's original righteousness. That is, the first man was created without sin (although he had the ability to sin). This is why the New Testament refers to Adam as "the son of God" (Luke 3:38); he was the bearer of God's image in the glory of righteousness. How much we have lost through sin. Yet Christian men, reborn through the grace of God, are declared holy—not in the sense of being perfect, but in the sense of being set apart for God, just as Adam was in the garden prior to sin. In that sense, as I indicated above, those who have been saved by Christ have the ability and the calling to represent God to the world in ways that unsaved people do not.

THE CHRISTIAN'S CALL TO REVEAL GOD

Understanding these three ways in which we bear God's image equips us for a life of obedience, as we seek to carry out our call to represent God to the world.

Paul speaks of our new nature in Christ being "renewed in knowledge after the image of its creator" (Col. 3:10). The context for that statement is Paul's exhortation for Christians to put away our sins: "anger, wrath, malice, slander, and obscene talk from your mouth" (Col. 3:8). He adds, "Do not lie to one another, seeing that you have put off the old self with its practices" (3:9). In short, the truest way that we bear God's image is by the practical righteousness that enables us to be more and more like God in our attitude and conduct. "Be holy," God says, "for I am holy" (Lev. 11:44), succinctly defining the moral dimension of bearing His image.

A Christian man is to know and glorify God in a life that is organized around his work (the previous chapter), himself (this chapter), and his relationships (subsequent chapters). We are called to bear God's image as His redeemed people, and what could be more exciting? Therefore, the great issues of our lives are not the amassing of personal fortunes (which others will receive after we die), not the enjoyment of maximum pleasure and recreation while we can (which substitutes the worship of self for the worship of God), and not the accumulation of earthly power (which we must lose in the end). The single greatest issue of our lives is this: revealing the glory of God to a sin-darkened world so that He will be praised and that lost sinners will be saved by coming to know the Lord. The great purpose of our lives is to reveal the glory and grace of God both by what we do and by who we are.

Revealing God by What We Do

What a difference it makes when a Christian man realizes that he does not have to be a fighter pilot, a movie star, or a pro athlete to have a life of significance and value. The world would have us believe that we really are nobodies unless we do something that gains worldly approval and generates worldly excitement. Sadly, I have known many Christian men who felt like losers because they were never war heroes, sports stars, or corporate titans. Against this way of thinking (really, this idolatry), I submit the case of Lawrence Dow, servant of Christ.

I first met Lawrence Dow on the night of my conversion to faith in Christ. He was a deacon at Tenth Presbyterian Church in Philadelphia, and that day he was greeting at the door before the evening service. I remember how his joyful demeanor made me feel accepted and welcome. During the years that followed, I got to know Lawrence pretty well, and his picture now sits on a bookshelf across from my desk. He reminds me of what one humble man can do to reveal the glory and grace of God to the world.

To tell about Lawrence, I only have to describe his funeral, following his death after a long struggle with cancer. Well before the service was scheduled to begin, our church sanctuary was jam-packed and there were parking problems throughout that downtown Philadelphia neighborhood. People must have wondered whether the president was in town or whether someone important—you know, a politician or a CEO—had died and was being buried. No, it was just Lawrence, a lively, elderly African American man, who never had a good formal education, worked as a doorman at a downtown hotel, and lived with his family in what other people call a ghetto.

Lawrence's funeral service was not only packed, it was long. Person after person came to bear testimony of how Lawrence had been used by God in their lives. Some had come to faith in Christ through Lawrence and were then mentored by him in their early Christian growth. In fact, three different ministers spoke about how Lawrence had led them to Christ and encouraged them in their service to their Lord. Lawrence's children and grandchildren spoke of his legacy of faith and love in their lives. The whole service was simply overwhelming.

Afterward, I was sitting in the office of one of my fellow ministers at the church. We were both dazed by what we had just seen, even though we both knew Lawrence well. The funeral had been a glorious experience and we were awestruck. After several minutes of silence, my friend said to me, "It just goes to show what God can do in the life of any man who yields himself unreservedly to Jesus." That is exactly what Lawrence's life of humble, godly service shows, and his story should encourage us to find our significance in revealing God's glory and grace through what we do as Christian men.

So what did Lawrence Dow do, and what should we do as bearers of God's image in this world? One answer is that Lawrence was utterly devoted to the work of the gospel. He looked on the world and on people through a biblical lens. He did not see rich or poor, black or white, high or low. He saw sinners who needed to be saved. He saw people broken by guilt who needed to hear about forgiveness. He saw people weakened in the bondage of sin who needed strength from the Lord. He devoted himself to the ministry of these things: salvation through faith in Jesus, forgiveness through the message of Christ's gospel, spiritual strength through prayer and God's Word. Lawrence had time for spiritual matters, and these were the things that interested him. He focused on the ministry of Christian truth and love to the people God brought into his life.

So what does this mean for the average Christian guy? It means that you need to get into the game—not a sports game on television, but the true and real contest for souls that is going on all around you. It means you should devote yourself to strengthening your own faith and drawing near to God so you can be used to strengthen others. It means you should be involved in your church by using whatever gifts the Lord has given you. It means you should be ready and open to be a spiritual blessing to people whom God will bring into your life. It means that when you meet someone who is down, you should encourage him or her with truth from God's Word. It means that when you find someone who is confused, you should come alongside to point out the way he should go. It means you should start noticing not just where people stand in the pecking order, but what is going on with them as individuals, and then minister gospel truth and Christlike love to them as those in need of grace.

Let me give some for-instances of how regular Christian guys can reveal God's glory to the world. Let's say someone moves into your neighborhood. This is an opportunity to display Christ. Start praying for that person and take advantage of opportunities to reach out. Maybe have the new guy (or his whole family) over for a meal and see what the Lord may do with it. Perhaps nothing will happen at first, but he will have learned that you are a caring Christian, and when he recognizes his spiritual needs, he may come to you. Or maybe he will accept your invitation to visit your church and will come to faith in Christ. Then you can encourage him in his growth.

Here's another for-instance. Let's say you have a friend who is making some bad choices. Instead of standing by and doing nothing, you approach your friend and express your concern, offering to meet him for prayer and Bible study. Again, he may reject you. But often such a person will praise God that someone noticed his need for friendship and help. So you encourage him in his time of weakness and need, and in so doing you make a decisive difference in his life while reminding him of God's love. In so doing, you bear God's image to him and minister God's glory in this world.

Every Christian man is called to get involved in God's work in some way. I like to think of it as going into "the family business." When the world was first created, God called Adam to enter into his labor, making the original garden more fruitful and spreading its bounty in the world. In our day, God's work in this world is the work of His gospel, the spreading of His saving grace in the lives of lost sinners.

This is what Jesus said when the Pharisees doubted Him: "The works that the Father has given me to accomplish, the very works that I am doing, bear witness about me that the Father has sent me" (John 5:36). Do you see the Lord's point here? Jesus said that He was revealing the truth about God by doing the works His Father sent Him to do, namely, the ministry of gospel truth and love in this world. Likewise, as servants of Jesus, we are to enter into this grace-bearing work, with the result that we will be drawn closer in our own relationship to God and we will show the glory of God to the world. Even though we are small, insignificant people in the eyes of the world—as Lawrence Dow certainly was—we can lead lives of stunning significance by revealing the image of God through our gospel labors in the name of Christ.

Revealing God by Who We Are

I have a lot of favorite Bible verses, but one that especially inspires me is 2 Corinthians 3:18, where Paul writes: "We all, with unveiled face, beholding the glory of the Lord, are being transformed into the same image from one degree of glory to another. For this comes from the Lord who is the Spirit."

This section of 2 Corinthians makes reference to Moses' experience of God, and in this particular passage we are reminded that we have a greater privilege than Moses did. Most importantly, we have a fuller understanding of the finished work of Jesus the Messiah and what it means to be saved. This verse identifies a particular outworking of our salvation that Moses was unable to enjoy.

After spending time with God on Mount Sinai, Moses wore a veil over his face when meeting with the Israelites because of the power of the glory of God that shone from his face. Over time, however, that glory faded. Yet under the new covenant, this dynamic is actually reversed. Like Moses, we behold the glory of God in the light of His Word. But unlike Moses, our glory from God only increases, as we "are being transformed into the same image from one degree of glory to another." God is increasingly working His own glory into us degree after degree, and He is doing this by the ministry of the Holy Spirit, whom God has sent to make us increasingly holy.

One of the most exciting things in my life is my growth in holiness, called *sanctification*, which the Bible identifies as the glory of God in me. I look back on the man I was ten years ago and, while there remains plenty of room for improvement, I can see how God has been working. In fact, I'm a little embarrassed of the man I was ten years ago, and I look forward ten years from now to being a little embarrassed of the man I am today. How exciting that God is working in me with the power of His Holy Spirit, to make me more like Him. What I am now is not all there is—praise the Lord. There is increased glory ahead for me, as God works in me through His Word and through prayer by the power of His mighty Spirit.

The New Testament says that Christians are "to be conformed to the image of his Son, in order that he might be the firstborn among many brothers" (Rom. 8:29). How does this happen? How are we transformed from one degree of glory to another? The Bible identifies three key resources, called "means of grace," which God has promised to bless in the lives of believing men and women, with the result that we will grow spiritually. These are God's Word, prayer, and the sacraments. To grow in Christlikeness and to enjoy more of the blessings of our salvation, Christians must make devoted use of these means of grace.

Transformation through God's Word. The priority of personal Bible study is seen in Paul's very first exhortation in his longest letter, Romans: "Do not be conformed to this world, but be transformed by the renewal of your mind, that by testing you may discern what is the will of God, what is good and acceptable and perfect" (Rom. 12:2). There really is no substitute for the regular practice of meeting with God in His Word, to be taught of Him and to meditate on His glorious truth. The very first psalm states that when a man delights in God's Word, meditating on it daily, he becomes "like a tree planted by streams of water that yields its fruit in its season, and its leaf does not wither. In all that he does, he prospers" (Ps. 1:3). Few things will more powerfully impact any man than a life of serious devotion to the Bible, through which God's life-giving Word enlightens our minds and hearts (Ps. 19:7–11). Jesus emphasized a commitment to Scripture in the most urgent terms: "If you abide in my word, you are truly my disciples, and you will know the truth, and the truth will set you free" (John 8:31–32).

Transformation through Prayer. A life committed to prayer is likewise essential for any man's spiritual growth. It is virtually impossible to find a man greatly used by God who is not strongly devoted to prayer. This means of grace is especially vital in receiving God's power to change our hearts and remove vestiges of sin. This is what Jesus had in mind when He promised that "everyone who asks receives, and the one who seeks finds, and to the one who knocks it will be opened" (Luke 11:10). Jesus was not speaking here of prayers for our sports teams. Rather, He was referring to God's power that is readily available to believers who seek for grace to turn from sin and grow in godly character. This is why Jesus concluded the teaching by saying, "how much more will the heavenly Father give the Holy Spirit to those who ask him!" (Luke 11:13). When we open our hearts to the Lord in prayer, desiring to be more like Christ and asking Him to show us areas in need of sanctification, God is faithful to provide the spiritual power needed to grow us in grace.

At the risk of too much self-disclosure, let me share an experience from early in my Christian life. In my Army days, I picked up the nasty habit of chewing tobacco. I started chewing in part because I needed stimulation for the physical demands of military service, especially the multiple days without sleep that commanders often endure. I also had the dumb idea that chewing was manly and cool. By the time I was thirty, the age at which I was converted to faith in Christ, I was seriously addicted. Within a few years, God called me into the ministry, so I resigned from the Army to attend seminary. Yet I was still chewing tobacco as a seminary student.

Burdened by the reality that this addiction had great power over me, aware of the health risks, and wanting to avoid the embarrassment of being a "dipping" preacher, I threw all my willpower at quitting tobacco. I could go cold-turkey and make it for weeks without chewing. But sooner or later, in a time of fatigue, frustration, or self-indulgence, I would steer my car into the convenience-store parking lot and drive away a few minutes later in guilty possession of another small, round container. It soon became clear to me that on my own I simply could not quit for good. Nicotine was in my flesh, not just as a physical addiction but as a moral need. I loved it, even though I hated it, and I simply could not will myself to leave it behind.

Of course, thanks to the indwelling sin that comes to us courtesy of Adam (as if you or I could have done any better), deep-rooted sin issues are tragically common, even among Christian men. What do we do when we have an issue we cannot beat? Don't you have one? Perhaps it is anger, envy, pride, laziness, or lust and pornography? Can we just will ourselves to Christlikeness? No! We are simply too weak and sin is too strong. We lack the power to rise above our flesh on our own—even as believers, and even with the Word of God in our hearts.

So what can we do once we have admitted we are slaves to a particular sin? As God's beloved children through faith in Christ, we can turn to the Lord in prayer. That is what I finally did. "Lord, I know that you desire me to quit using tobacco," I prayed. "But I lack the power to do so. In the name of Christ, would you deliver me from this addiction? Would you please weaken my evil desires and give me the strength to resist for good? Would you set me free once and for all so I can be more like Jesus?" This is how we should pray with respect to all of sin's bondage in our hearts. Prayer like this is an essential means of grace for our deliverance from sin and our growth in Christlikeness.

It is precisely this kind of scenario that the New Testament has in mind when it teaches, "if we ask anything according to his will he hears us" (1 John 5:14). When it comes to praying against sin, God's will is no mystery. He has told us that His agenda is our Christlikeness, for Paul says simply, "This is the will of God, your sanctification" (1 Thess. 4:3). We can therefore know beyond any question that when we pray for greater sanctification we are praying in God's will. As we ask the Lord for grace to become more like Christ, we may be absolutely certain of receiving that grace.

So it was that God delivered me from the addiction of chewing tobacco. God did not enable me merely to cope with this addiction. Instead, over a period of time during which He called me to be persistent in prayer, the Lord removed the addiction. This was quite a learning experience for me. Since then, I have prayed for numerous issues of personal sanctification and have experienced God's power at work through the Holy Spirit, enabling me to grow in grace and godliness. James' dictum about prayer is true especially for the spiritual resources for growth in grace: "You do not have, because you do not ask" (James 4:2). For, Jesus promised, "the heavenly Father give[s] the Holy Spirit to those who ask him!" (Luke 11:13).

Transformation through the Sacraments. Finally, the Lord has given the sacrament of baptism and especially the recurring sacrament of the Lord's Supper (communion) as means of grace. Jesus instituted the Lord's Supper as a perpetual ordinance for His disciples until He returns, saying, "Do this in remembrance of me" (Luke 22:19). The Lord's Supper does not function by any magic in the formula of words or in the elements themselves, but the Holy Spirit strengthens the faith of those who commune with Jesus, as we receive the elements that signify His death for our sins. "The cup of blessing that we bless," Paul writes, "is it not a participation in the blood of Christ? The bread that we break, is it not a participation in the body of Christ?" (1 Cor. 10:16). Our participation is spiritual, not material, through faith in God's Word and by the power of the Holy Spirit, who nourishes our faith as we commune with Christ.

THE PROMISE OF FINAL VICTORY

As we avail ourselves of these three means of grace, God will free us from some persistent sins quickly. Release from others may require a considerably longer time. Some sins will undoubtedly be with us until death, for no man achieves perfect holiness in this life (Phil. 3:12). But how wonderful then that, as we rise from these mortal bodies to be with the Lord forever, we will leave behind us all those remaining areas of corruption. The gradual process of being freed from sin in this life, which is our calling in God, will be crowned on the day of our death with that total victory that will be ours by virtue of being in Christ. The day of our death will be the day that we commit our last sin, but until then our calling and our destiny in Christ is to become increasingly holy as we grow in the knowledge of God and the practice of godliness.

There can be no higher calling and no greater privilege in this life than to cooperate with God in being further conformed to His image. And there is one more benefit: by growing in godliness and grace, we prepare ourselves for the glories that will be ours in eternity through our faith in Jesus. As Paul liked to say, "To him be glory forever and ever" (Rom. 11:36; 16:7; Gal. 1:5; Eph. 3:21; Phil. 4:20; 1 Tim. 1:17). The Lord now calls Christian men to so live that our chief end in life is to glorify God and to enjoy knowing Him forever.

Questions for Reflection and Discussion

- When you think of the glory of God, what comes to mind? How does nature reveal God's glory? In what ways is man especially created to display the glory of God?

- How did God's original design enable Adam to bear God's image? How has sin kept us from glorifying God as we should? How does the grace of Christ enable us to glorify God?

- Do you think your life has real significance? If not, why not? Why is it that God's calling for us in Christ makes our lives truly significant? How might God be calling you to be more active in spreading the glory of His truth and grace in Christ?

- If someone were to ask ten people who know you well, what would they say is the area in which you most need spiritual growth and improvement? How would you answer this question? Have you tried to improve through your own power? How would you go about seeking God's power to enable you to advance in Christlikeness?

Chapter 5

MAN AS SHEPHERD-LORD

This is the last chapter of doctrinal groundwork before we move on to practical application. So let's do a quick recap of what we have learned so far about the biblical model of manhood. We have been drawing our picture of masculinity from the opening chapters of Genesis, and so far we have noted the following:

- God made man in His own image.
- God placed man in the garden, the world of God's covenantal relationships.
- God placed him in the garden that he might work and be fruitful.
- Toward that end, God gave man the work-and-keep mandate of cultivating and protecting.
- The ultimate goal—the chief end of man—is that he might display God's glory in the world.

In making these points, we have noted man's call to dominion, that is, the call to exercise authority on God's behalf in the world. This is nothing less than a call to exercise lordship.

THE LEADER AS LORD

While this call was given generally to man and woman (Gen. 1:26), we see in Genesis 2 that it was distinctively the man's role to exercise lordship in God's garden-world. God was the Lord and Adam was the lord (note the small *l*) whom God placed in the garden as His deputy. The best way to see this is to note how God granted to Adam the right to name the other creatures, naming being a function of lordship:

> Out of the ground the LORD God formed every beast of the field and every bird of the heavens and brought them to the man to see what he would call them. And whatever the man called every living creature, that was its name. The man gave names to all livestock and to the birds of the heavens and to every beast of the field. (Gen. 2:19–20)

Notice how the Lord brought all the animals and birds to the man, so that they answered to Adam. From that point, their identity reflected Adam's lordship; they bore the names assigned to them by the highest of all God's creatures. Adam was God's ordained servant as lord of the garden, just as men today are to be God's servants in our exercise of authority. *Lordship*—or, as we would say it today, *leadership*—is intrinsic to the male calling in the world.

Sometimes the word *lordship* can rankle us. We easily associate the word either with God (a good reason to rankle) or with images of overfed men in castles wearing powdered wigs and strange clothing. But God calls all men to exercise leadership (lordship) within some sphere of life—at home through marriage and fatherhood, in the workplace, in the church, and in society in general. It is of the greatest urgency that men understand and embrace a biblical idea of leadership.

LEADERSHIP: A CRISIS AND A PRIORITY

Whatever we call it, it seems obvious that America is facing a leadership crisis. Bold leadership and the exercise of authority are commonly met with skepticism, if not outright disdain. I believe this is happening for two reasons. First, in our sinful pride we all have a resistance to being led, especially in a country like America, where independence is highly prized. Second, we are all familiar with leaders who have used their power to enrich their own lives, abusing rather than blessing those entrusted to their care. Some business leaders have been shown to be self-serving scoundrels, so we tend to see all of them in that light. Political leaders are widely perceived, rightly or wrongly, as having been bought by moneyed interests. Because so many men fail to conduct themselves in an honorable, biblical way, women can become skeptical of the entire male gender. Certainly, few of our cultural heroes today are leaders in the biblical sense—those who serve and influence their followers, steering them toward some greater good.

There is therefore an urgent, vital need in our world today

for men who are leaders in the truest sense of the word. Scripture provides examples to inspire us and precepts to guide us as we seek to become lords under God's higher lordship, leaders who are servants of God and of His cherished people. God gives such leadership as a way for His blessing to come to earth. He is faithful to provide such servant leaders for His people, and He calls Christian men to exercise lordship on His behalf (Eph. 4:11–13; 1 Peter 5:1–5). Will we answer that call? As David sang at the end of his life: "When one rules justly over men, ruling in the fear of God, he dawns on them like the morning light, like the sun shining forth on a cloudless morning, like rain that makes grass to sprout from the earth" (2 Sam. 23:3–4).

THE LEADER AS SHEPHERD

If there is one image in the Bible that sums up God's model for leadership, it is that of the shepherd watching over, protecting, and leading his flock of sheep. We find this idea from the earliest days of God's people. While the Bible does not tell us that Adam became a shepherd, we do see him in Genesis 2 as lord over the animals, and his first godly son, Abel, is specifically identified as "a keeper of sheep" (Gen. 4:2).

Abraham, Isaac, and Jacob were all herdsmen, and Moses was "keeping the flock of his father-in-law Jethro" when he saw the burning bush and was called by God to lead Israel (Ex. 3:1). Moses prayed, "May the Lord appoint over the congregation one to lead them out and bring them in, so they will not be like sheep who have no shepherd" (Num. 27:17). The Old Testament's ideal leader, King David—from whom we have much to learn—was famous as the shepherd-king of Israel. Psalm 78:72 says of David, "With upright heart he shepherded them and guided them with his skillful hand." Most importantly, Jesus picked up this biblical image to depict His own servant lordship: "I am the good shepherd" (John 10:11). So all through the Bible, from beginning to end, God's model of servant lordship is that of the shepherd-leader.

The true shepherd-leader fulfills his role in a way that evokes feelings of security among those who are led. Such a shepherd lives among the sheep, identifying with them in his heart and sharing their hardships, risks, and dangers. Perhaps most important is the radical way the shepherd looks upon his sheep. Today we are accustomed to leaders who use their followers, seeking only personal or organizational gain from the flock. But a true shepherd's attention and passion are directed toward the well-being of the sheep themselves. The sheep are his preoccupation, his burden, and his joy. To be sure, a leader is responsible to ensure that his people work hard and well, and financial realities may require a business to reduce its workforce. But within organizational constraints and requirements, a true leader is devoted to his flock and they know it. This is why young David, watching over his flocks at night, rejoiced at the thought that the Lord was his own shepherd: "The LORD is my shepherd; I shall not want" (Ps. 23:1).

The shepherd-leader wearies himself in sacrificial labor for the sake of his sheep. It is when the sheep have grown strong, when the flock has survived the hazards of its journey, returning to the village transformed from lambs into strong rams, that the shepherd has faithfully discharged his duty. To be sure, sheep have to be motivated to keep moving and must often be chastised to stay out of trouble. But it is the sheep themselves who fill the shepherd's thoughts as he slips into sleep at night, and it is for them that his eyes search when first light signals each new day. The shepherd is the servant of the sheep; it is their growth and nurture that set the agenda for his success.[6]

The way for Christian men to leave a lasting legacy is for us to embrace the Bible's model of shepherd-leadership. Our goal must be not just to carve out success for ourselves, but to leave a blessed imprint on the lives of those who are under our care. This can happen only when we as shepherds are ready to give our lives for the sheep, as did Jesus, our Good Shepherd. He said, "The good shepherd lays down his life for the sheep" (John 10:11). Christian leaders must likewise learn to measure our success in the security and inspiration of those who follow us, in their growing confidence and ability, and in the achievements of others rather than our own. Toward the end of his life, the apostle John wrote in this manner, saying, "I have **no greater joy** than to hear that my children are walking in the truth" (3 John 4).

SHEPHERD-LEADERSHIP
AND THE MASCULINE MANDATE

Not surprisingly, the model of the leader as shepherd fits perfectly the work-and-keep Masculine Mandate of Genesis 2:15. God placed Adam in the garden to *work* it—to make it grow—and shepherds are leaders who nurture and inspire the hearts of those who follow. God also called Adam to *keep* the garden—to stand guard over it—and it is the shepherd-leader who protects those under his charge, keeping one eye always on the flock and the other alert for predators. Good shepherd-leadership, then, will always resemble Adam's servant-lordship as the flock, like a garden, grows and bears fruit of all kinds under the watchful protection of the shepherd.

David's tribute to God's shepherd-leadership in Psalm 23 presents the components of this role in inspiring detail. "The LORD is my shepherd," he rejoices, "I shall not want" (v. 1). The psalm continues as an outline of the kind of shepherding care God provides and that He desires from those who exercise authority in His name. As David reflects on a shepherd's ministry to the sheep, he sees a depiction of God's ministry to him—and our calling in shepherd-leadership—as including three main tasks: guiding (echoing Adam's call to work the garden), and protecting and caring (echoing Adam's call to keep it).

Work: Shepherding as Guiding

When David rejoices, "I shall not want," it is largely because of the guidance he receives from God: "He makes me lie down in green pastures. He leads me beside still waters. . . . He leads me in paths of righteousness for his name's sake" (Ps. 23:2–3). For sheep, of course, life is all about having grazing grounds that are safe and lush, that can be arrived at and returned from safely, and that have fresh water nearby. The shepherd does not stumble upon such locations by accident. He must study the landscape and search out the safest routes to the best grazing grounds. Likewise, a shepherd-leader of a family, church, or business must be able to point his followers in the right direction and guide them safely.

This kind of sound guidance requires competence in whatever endeavor one is pursuing. A young tank officer, for example, may be a caring commander, but this will mean little if he is not also an able tactician and competent in the myriad tasks necessary to fulfill his role. Effective leadership always requires the leader to devote himself to acquiring the competence necessary to guide his particular flock. The most necessary competence of any leader is a knowledge of God's truth in the Bible. How is a father and husband, for example, to guide his family without a knowledge of the Bible's teaching on marriage, raising children, handling money, serving in the church, and more?

Referring to one of the principal forms of guidance in ancient Israel, the wise man said, "Where there is no prophetic vision the people cast off restraint, but blessed is he who keeps the law" (Prov. 29:18). Indeed, it is when leaders are too lazy or self-absorbed to learn and apply truth that the Bible's lament comes to pass: "they were harassed and helpless, like sheep without a shepherd" (Matt. 9:36).

To be successful as a shepherd-leader, a man must master the needed skills, primary among them the study of the truth of God's Word.

Keep: Shepherding as Protecting

David also notes the value of the shepherd's protective rule over the sheep, particularly in the shadow of danger: "Even though

I walk through the valley of the shadow of death, I will fear no evil, for you are with me" (Ps. 23:4). This reminds us that true leadership is always personal. It is the presence of an individual—his protective shepherd—that gives David confidence despite the looming presence of danger. The shepherd will not permit any threat or adversity to tear him down or cancel the blessings already received.

We can well imagine a flock of skittish sheep passing through a dark canyon, with crags and boulders on each side that could conceal a lurking wolf. At the slightest sound, the sheep recoil in apprehension, unable to move forward, until their searching gaze rests upon the comforting figure of the shepherd. His personal presence, watching over and protecting them, gives the sheep assurance, calming them and moving them forward because of their trust in his watchful care. The sheep can go forward with a sense of comfort because they have confidence that their shepherd will preserve and protect them.

The shepherd's presence includes the unmistakable symbols of his authority by which he protects his flock: "Your rod and your staff, they comfort me" (Ps. 23:4). These were the tools of the shepherd's trade and the emblems of his position. The purpose of the long staff, with its crooked head, was to slip around wayward necks, coaxing strays back onto the safe path, lest they be harmed. It symbolized the leadership authority given to the shepherd. Followers rightly expect leaders to enforce proper rules and shape godly behaviors. Indeed, especially in times of trouble and danger, follower-sheep are comforted by a trustworthy shepherd who faithfully wields protective authority, thus maintaining order within the flock.

The purpose of the rod—a short, blunt weapon used to fend off aggressive predators—was protective in a more forceful way. Just as sheep took comfort to see the shepherd with his rod, men and women today look to faithful leaders to wield their God-given office to protect and defend. What was true for the sheep then is true for all of us now: "Your rod and your staff, they comfort me."

Work and Keep: Shepherding as Caring

As David concludes Psalm 23, there is a noteworthy shift in his language. Starting in verse 5, in which he looks with thanks to God for blessings that await us in heaven, David leaves the metaphor of sheep and speaks more directly of human needs and blessings. We may summarize his concluding praise to the Lord as involving God's ministry of caring—leadership bringing together both working and keeping. In these concluding verses, we find David emphasizing provision, acceptance, blessing, and belonging.

Provision and Acceptance. David first describes God's care with a vivid metaphor: "You prepare a table before me in the presence of my enemies" (Ps. 23:5). This idea of a table—sharing a meal—involves the provision of nourishment in a context of unqualified acceptance. As the Lord spreads His table before us, those who have been invited into His household, we are graciously accepted and given sustenance. As shepherd-lords seeking to imitate our Father, we must first of all be fully accepting of those sheep God has called us to lead and make sure they are aware of that fact.

Blessing. David then adds, "You anoint my head with oil; my cup overflows" (Ps. 23:5). Entering a home in dry and dusty Palestine, soothing oil for the face and head was a choice blessing. So also was the cup which overflowed with wine, refreshing the parched throat of the sojourner. Rather than following the American stereotype of cold, macho masculinity, Christian men should seek to grow in their ability genuinely to bless others.

Belonging. This leads to the psalm's final verse: "Surely goodness and mercy shall follow me all the days of my life, and I shall dwell in the house of the LORD forever" (Ps. 23:6). Providing a true sense of belonging is one of the most caring gifts any leader can give to a follower. This is especially true when our witness of the gospel brings people into the eternal blessing of belonging as a member of God's house.

SHEPHERDING AS SELF-SACRIFICE

In Psalm 23, we are reminded of the ultimate reason for keeping the sheep safe: God has a destination for us. It is a place of blessing, provision, and acceptance, a place where we belong, permanently and irrevocably. The certainty that every true Christian will dwell in this place of unending goodness and mercy should fill our hearts with joy. For everything God has done has positioned and prepared us to enjoy him forever. Before we conclude this chapter we must, therefore, look to the single most important of these redemptive acts of

God—because it offers us the single most important example of what it means to be a shepherd-lord.

In looking to God as his Shepherd, David saw both love and self-sacrifice, and he rejoiced. Jesus, of course, brought divine love and self-sacrifice to their ultimate fruition. Anticipating His death on the cross to deliver His flock safely into heaven, He said, "The good shepherd lays down his life for the sheep" (John 10:11). The sacrificial work of Christ on the cross is the ultimate act of "keeping," because in it the gains of God's blessing were secured and the battle won.

Just as God calls Christian men to bear His image before the world, He calls us to imitate Him as His servant-lords in the world. We would do well to pay the closest attention to the ultimate Shepherd-Lord, Christ Himself, in His ultimate act of service to His sheep: His death on the cross. For just as Jesus' shepherding care caused Him to lay down His life, our shepherd-leadership will call for immense self-sacrifice. Our reward? The rich satisfaction of being greatly used by God in the lives of His sheep and, to varying degrees, the "unfading crown of glory" (1 Peter 5:4) that Jesus has prepared for all who have faithfully shepherded the beloved flock that He purchased with His own blood.

Questions for Reflection and Discussion

- The author states that our times suffer from a crisis of leadership. Do you agree or disagree? How can Christian men provide one answer to the leadership crisis of our times?

- Why were so many of the Bible's great leaders shepherds? What does the shepherd motif say about God's attitude toward His people? How would you compare shepherd-leadership to other common forms of leadership today?

- How can you begin practicing shepherd-leadership, regardless of your life setting? What are the biggest changes this will require in your treatment of other people?

- Are you prepared to serve as a shepherd-leader? Do you have the needed competence to guide others? Are you able to exercise ruling authority to guide and protect? Are you interested in caring ministry, like that which Jesus gives to His people? In what ways does this description of leadership challenge you for growth?

Part Two

LIVING OUR
MANDATE

Chapter 6

GOD'S ASTONISHING DESIGN FOR MARRIAGE

Knowing makes all the difference. Take computer passwords, for example. If you don't know a particular password and can't find it out, there usually isn't much you can do. Knowing is vital for driving directions, too. Get one little step wrong, and you may wind up lost and bewildered in a place you never intended to visit.

As Christians, we are convinced of the importance of knowing, and we believe that Scripture contains the most important things that can be known. In fact, having an accurate grasp of biblical truth is essential for how we live. In this chapter we begin discussing some of the most practical of these essential truths: those concerning the vital institution of marriage.

As I have emphasized in this book, Genesis 2 shows that God created man for a purpose. God ordained that Adam would bear His image both in his person and in his work, and God put Adam in the world to work it and keep it—to be a cultivator and a protector. This divine mandate for men applies to all our roles and relationships, including being fathers to our children, friends to other men, and servants in the church. But more primary than any of these is the Masculine Mandate as it applies to the covenant of marriage, which God has made basic to all human society and which most closely resembles our relationship with Him. When it comes to marriage, knowing definitely makes all the difference.

What do men need to know about marriage? If my experience as a pastor and counselor is any guide—experience corroborated by nearly every pastor with whom I have discussed this topic—the best answer is something like this: "Quite a bit more than they know now." For there is unquestionably a general ignorance among Christians, most significantly among Christian men, about the Bible's teaching on marriage.

It is often surprising, sometimes amazing, and occasionally shocking just how little most men really know about marriage. I have often heard, especially from someone who had been divorced years earlier, "If only I'd realized this when I was younger!" Even though all the basic answers about marriage are provided by God right in Genesis 2, it seems that most men have little or no idea what marriage is about, how it is designed by God, or what its purpose is to be in our lives.

If men do not get their guidance about marriage from the Bible, where does it come from? There is certainly little of value to be gained from secular society, which is hopelessly confused and deceived about most relational matters. Even in the church, there sometimes are few role models approximating the biblical ideal. This is why I am taking three chapters to explore men's calling in marriage—one of the great callings in all of life and the relationship in which our Masculine Mandate has its most intimate and potent expression.

DESIGNED INCOMPLETE

All through the Bible's creation account, we read that what God had created "was good." Having made it all Himself, God was pleased with everything He saw, declaring seven times in Genesis 1 that it was either "good" or "very good." Suddenly, though, we see that God discovered something that was not as good as it ought to be. What an extraordinary thing. God looked on His creation and declared that it needed an improvement. What was wrong? It was not a flaw in God's creation design, not some mistake or failure on His part, but something that remained incomplete. God looked at the very pinnacle of His creation, the man who bore His image, and declared, "It is *not good* that the man should be alone" (Gen. 2:18, emphasis added).

This is where the Bible's teaching on marriage begins, with *the man's need for a partner.* God looked on Adam in the garden, saw him alone, and said, "This is not good." God says the same thing about single adult men today. He looks into their apartments and refrigerators and sighs, "Not good." More importantly, God looks into our hearts and our characters, and says: "I have made man to be in partnership with a woman. It does not work very well when a man remains unmarried." My point is not to rebuke adult men who are unmarried, but simply to point out the truth of God's Word. When it comes to the physical, emotional, spiritual, and sexual well-being of a man, it is not good for him to be alone.

After making this observation, God immediately began to turn this "not good" into a "very good" for Adam. But first God made a point. We read this:

> So out of the ground the LORD God formed every beast of the field and every bird of the heavens and brought them to the man to see what he would call them. And whatever the man called every living creature, that was its name. The man gave names to all livestock and to the birds of the heavens and to every beast of the field. But for Adam there was not found a helper fit for him. (Gen. 2:19–20)

What an experience this must have been for Adam. Every manner of creature was paraded before him for his inspection and naming (exercising his lordship over them). We can imagine him riding the first horse, wrestling with the first lion, swimming with the first dolphin, and (best of all, of course) playing with the first dog. To name them, Adam needed to study them, and based on his intimate experience, he declared the sounds that would go with each kind of creature. What a thrill this must have been. Yet, according to the Lord, in one sense the exercise was a massive failure: "But for Adam there was not found a helper fit for him" (Gen. 2:20).

This statement makes an essential point that every man needs to take to heart: *you and I are designed incomplete.* Men are made by God not to stand in isolation but in need of companionship, and the one companion who fulfills God's intention in our lives is a woman. We do not find completion through our job only, important as a man's work is. We do not become whole through our male friendships, however great it may feel to "hang out with the guys." A dog may provide a certain kind of companionship (I write these words with my chocolate lab curled up at my feet), but a dog cannot be a true companion to any man. We say that a dog is "man's best friend," but God doesn't think so. The only way a man can fellowship with a dog is by stooping to the dog's level, which is fine on occasion, but not as the basic rule of a man's life. God intends for man to have a partner who bears God's image along with man, and who with man can look upward to God and live for Him.

There is also an important point to be seen in God's use of the word *helper*. A wife is indeed the best possible companion for a man, but God did not call Eve a "companion" to Adam because that would suggest the primary purpose of mankind on this earth is fellowship and relational fulfillment. In the same way, a wife is clearly and uniquely designed to be a mate to man, but God did not call Eve a "mate" to Adam because that would suggest our primary purpose is procreation and sexual pleasure. God said Adam needed a "helper" because it places the *primary* emphasis on the shared mandate to work and keep God's creation under the man's leadership. A wife is called to help her husband in this grand, glorious task in a myriad of ways—by enjoying fellowship and relational fulfillment as his companion, by enjoying sexual pleasure and bearing children as his mate, and on and on. But it all comes under the heading of "helping," which is essentially about the working and keeping of God's creation. In this book I will use many words to refer to a wife's relationship to her husband, depending on the context. None of these, however, contradict or replace her primary relationship as helper.

A MAN SHOULD FIND A WIFE

Before I go further, let me take a few moments to address single men. I said that I was not going to rebuke you for being unmarried, and I meant that. Moreover, I realize that it is not always so easy to find a godly wife, and that many earnestly seeking brothers have been greatly frustrated in this pursuit. Still, the Bible's teaching requires me to encourage you to realize how vitally important it is (in the vast majority of cases) that you become married. If you have shied away from marriage, let me urge you to reconsider and (perhaps) to commit to the necessary growing up. If you have tried but met only frustration, let me encourage you to renew your prayers to the Lord and keep at it.[7]

By God's design, as seen in Genesis 2, a man is completed by a woman, and not just any woman, but by a wife. From this it follows plainly: It is vital for the well-being of almost any adult man that he becomes married. It is true that the apostle Paul identified a "gift of singleness" that he wished all men had (1 Cor. 7:7). He was referring to the ability some men possess to devote themselves to serving God without the encumbrances of marriage. So, unless you have the gift Paul referred to, it is imperative for your well-being that you be married, to move beyond the "not good" status of single adulthood.

This is an especially important message for young adult men today, who are bombarded with the opposite message. "Dude, don't get married!" their friends all say. When the first guy gets married after college, his male friends lament the occasion as if he had contracted a fatal disease. So while God says, "It is not good for men to be alone," men tell each other to avoid marriage like the plague. As always, however, God is the one who is right. The best thing that a young Christian man can do—I mean one who is able to meet the obligations of marriage, which implies he should be eligible for full-time employment—is to marry a godly woman.

In my opinion, and in keeping with the Bible's teaching, one of the biggest problems in the church today is the failure of young adult men to value and pursue marriage. This problem is played out in the frustration of Christian women in their twenties, whose God-designed bodies scream, "Babies!" and whose God-designed emotional make-up is geared for marriage, but who find practically no Christian men in their peer group who are ready for or interested in marriage. As a result of a male culture that fears marriage, men in their twenties and thirties slide into sexual sin (marriage, after all, is God's provision for lust; see 1 Cor. 7:9) and cultivate antisocial behaviors that perpetuate emotional and social immaturity. Today, when God looks on single males and says, "Not good," He undoubtedly has in mind a long list of truly "unfit helpers," among them the pornography, video games, sports obsessions, and empty pizza boxes that are intrinsic to so many young adult male lives, even among Christians.

Our society tells young adult men to deprive themselves of God's provision for their physical, emotional, and sexual needs so they can remain as immature and self-absorbed as possible, for as long as possible. You know what the Bible says about this: it just is not good.

A HELPER SUITABLE, YET DIFFERENT

God made the woman not merely to be a helper to man, but also to be "fit" for him, a helper well-suited to her role. This comes from a word in the Hebrew language that is used in Scripture only in this passage: *kenegdo*. The root form of this word means "in front of" or "across from." The idea is that the woman corresponds to the man, not as a mirror image but as a puzzle piece that clicks. Consider how God made her:

> So the Lord God caused a deep sleep to fall upon the man, and while he slept took one of his ribs and closed up its place with flesh. And the rib that the LORD God had taken from the man he made into a woman and brought her to the man. Then the man said, "This at last is bone of my bones and flesh of my flesh; she shall be called Woman, because she was taken out of Man." (Gen. 2:21–23)

God took a part of Adam, so that the woman corresponded to him, but then God made her a little different, fashioning

82

Adam's rib into the woman. The word for "made" or "fashioned" indicates special artisanship, which we see in the beauty that women bring into men's lives. Because God made the woman from man and then fashioned her to be different, she is precisely fitted as a helper for man, and beautifully so.

Our society does not place high status on being a helper because of an irrational cultural emphasis on independence and autonomy. Yet being a helper is a noble thing in God's eyes. Furthermore, *helper* is the word the Bible uses most frequently to speak of God in His covenant faithfulness to His people. "The God of my father was my help," rejoiced Moses (Ex. 18:4), and one of the most helpful things God ever did was to make woman for man as his helper. What a help a godly wife is to any man.

I have an older friend whose dear wife of many decades recently died. His friends are now concerned that he may soon die, since she is no longer there to take care of him. His whole well-being—physical, emotional, sexual—resulted from her ministry to him. His effectiveness as a business leader largely depended on the care that she devoted to their home and to his personal life. Like many men of the older generation today, my friend has no idea how to cook, clean, or iron clothes. He was completely dependent on the loving and faithful help of his wife, and it is in large part because of the outstanding woman she was that he is the outstanding man he is. A husband's dependence on his wife is precisely as God designed it.

God has made women in such a way that they enjoy caring for a man and are not content without a man to love. This is why marriage is not merely the "necessary evil" some make it out to be, but rather that, as John Calvin writes, "woman is given as a companion and an associate to the man, to assist him to live well." Thus, he concludes, "marriage will really prove to men the best support of life."[8]

The Wonder and the Challenge

In God's fashioning of woman as a suitable helper for man, we find both the wonder of marriage and the challenge of marriage. By God's design, a woman is made for essential oneness with man. Thus, Adam cheered, "This at last is bone of my bones and flesh of my flesh; she shall be called Woman, because she was taken out of Man" (Gen. 2:23). Women are men's equals, not men's possessions or slaves. Yet they are different. So men find women compellingly attractive, yet mysterious.

Because the woman was made in a way that corresponds to the man, yet is different from the man, we can achieve deep union with our wives while never ceasing to discover new things about them. To be sure, the differences between men and women (which are fundamental and unchangeable because of God's creation) are such that a man will never really figure out his wife. I confess that after sixteen years of marriage I still struggle to understand the way my wife thinks and feels, not because of any deficiencies on her part, but simply because she is a woman. This is by God's design, since it allows the marriage relationship to be compelling, interesting, and demanding over the many decades of even the longest life.

Many a man rues the differences between himself and his

wife, especially as they are magnified by sin. Why does she like to *shop* for hours when it only takes a few minutes to *buy* what she needs? Why does she always want to talk about our relationship? Why doesn't she like my solutions, preferring instead to dwell on the problems? Why is it so hard to communicate and why is it sometimes difficult to get along?

Even apart from considerations of sin, the answer to all these questions is "God designed it this way." How helpful it is to know why and how God made the woman for man! The simple fact is that God did not design marriage to be like a group of guys hanging out. All men need is some pizza and a decent game to play or watch, and we can be pals. But throw in a woman and everything becomes so much harder. (It works the other way, too, although feminine society seems much more complicated.) Why, oh why? Because God intended it this way. God wants us as men to learn to give, serve, and love similar to the way He gives, serves, and loves. We were made to bear His image, after all, and the main classroom in which a Christian man learns to be like his heavenly Father is in the school of marriage.

Love Is Not Meant to be Easy

Let's put it in terms of the different kinds of love. The Bible uses four words for love. There is *storge*, which speaks of family love. (We have to love our family members.) There is also *eros*, which is sexual love. Then there is *philos*, which basically means "to like." This is the love that receives, and it is what men tend to have in mind when it comes to marriage. We tell our wives, "I love you," meaning, "You make *me* feel good," or "I like feeling this way because of you." That kind of circumstantial, self-focused love is what comes most easily to us. But God desires us to have the fourth kind of love, *agape*, which is the giving love that God has for us. When Paul says, "Husbands, love your wives" (Eph. 5:25), he uses *agape*.

God has so designed marriage that it doesn't always make us feel good. God desires that when a Christian man says to his wife, "I love you," he is not merely indicating, "you give to me," but he is also resolving, "I give to you." He loves her by giving himself to her and for her. Isn't this what God did for us in giving His only Son?

Just as God's gift of His Son was a costly gift, God intends for a man's love to his wife to be costly. Simply put, it is not easy for man to love his wife, and God does not intend it to be easy. If it were easy, it wouldn't be valuable. Instead, God desires us as husbands to love our wives who we don't fully understand, who think and feel differently than we do, and who require a love that involves sacrifice on our part. One of God's chief purposes in our lives as men is to teach us to love as He loves. His complementary design in marriage is intended to promote that God-like *agape* love in us.

This means it is neither necessary nor possible for a man to "figure out" his wife completely. God does not command men and women to be identical or to understand one another perfectly. It is by God's creation design that we think and feel differently. Those areas in which we fundamentally differ from one another will never change. Woman will always be similar to man *and* she will always be different from man. She is a helper, uniquely suited to complement him.

How to Love

What, then, is a man to do with the woman God has given him? The answer concludes the teaching of Genesis 2 on how a man is to love his wife: "Therefore a man shall leave his father and his mother and hold fast to his wife, and they shall become one flesh. And the man and his wife were both naked and were not ashamed" (Gen. 2:24–25).

In these verses, God calls man to take specific steps in the relationship as its leader. His wife, as his helper, is called to do the same, but God presents this directive to the man: he must "hold fast" to his wife. Older Bible versions render this as "cleave," which reminds us of sticking things together with glue. That is a good picture of what God intends between husband and wife. He wants us to bond to one another.

But bonding changes us. It requires us to give things up, to live differently than we did previously. Exactly! God did not make man to live for himself. God did not put Adam in the garden to be infatuated with his tools and his toys and his self-centered lifestyle. He put Adam there to work and keep, cultivating, nurturing, and protecting that which God had entrusted to him. And the first step for many of us in becoming the men God wants us to be is to become married, so that we will leave behind our selfish ways and begin fulfilling our masculine calling through our relationship with our wives. This is for our good, as any man in a godly marriage can tell you. It is great to have a helper designed by God to love and minister to me. But it is especially good to have to rise up in masculine virtue and strength for the sake of my wife, leaving behind a self-focus that was, at best, only intended for a temporary season of singleness.

From Genesis 2, we learn that an accurate view of marriage begins with recognizing God's intentions for men in marriage. We are called to find our satisfaction in working and keeping, most often having married and bonded to a woman God has given us as a suitable helper. And because God is good, he has made woman so that she finds much of her own fulfillment in being that helper.

As we saw earlier in this book, the chief good God intends for all His sons is that they should bear His image in spiritual strength and maturity. For the vast majority of men, this is impossible to do outside marriage with the fullness God intends. This is why it was "not good" for Adam to be alone. As the chief end of a man's life is to glorify God and enjoy knowing Him forever, the chief end of marriage is that a man and a woman should know and glorify God together through their lives, and most particularly through their godly love for one another.

Questions for Reflection and Discussion

- Why is it not good for a man to be alone? Why is the reluctance of young adult men to get married so dangerous? Why does God want men to enter into the marriage relationship?

- Why can't dogs really be "man's best friend"? What are God's goals in the companionship between a husband and wife? What does "suitable helper" mean?

- If you are a married man, what kind of "giving love" connects with your wife? Do you find this easy or difficult? Why is it a challenge for men to go beyond receiving love to the giving love that God desires? How might you pray so as to better bond with and minister to your wife?

- If you are single, what is keeping you from marriage? Pray for God to enable you to take a wife and for God to provide you with a wife.

Chapter 7

MARRIAGE CURSED AND REDEEMED

"Women are cursed." So muttered a friend back in college after the break-up of his most recent romance. "Women are cursed," we replied in a chorus of manly affirmation, reflecting on how those mysterious creatures never seemed to act as we wanted them to. This was why we found it easier to hang out with guys, why we so often treated women far worse than they deserved, and why we later tried to put off marriage as long as we could.

In reality, the fact that women are unfathomable to men is God's intended blessing for us, as we saw in the previous chapter. With that noted, my friend's statement should otherwise be accepted as true. Women *are* cursed. But then, so are men. And it is the curse that fell on men and women because of sin that makes marriage not only challenging but painfully impossible to so many people. Sin's curse on marriage is the best explanation for the sky-high divorce rate in America today. Even among Christians, the curse of God on men and women, and thus on marriage, is reflected in much bitterness, pain, and sin—and all of this from the institution that God gave for our blessing.

ADAM'S APPLE

Every Christian needs to be quite familiar with Genesis 3, the account of man's fall into sin, for it was in response to this fall that Jesus Christ came into the world to suffer and die for our salvation. The story begins in Genesis 2, where we learn that God commanded our first parents not to eat of the tree of the knowledge of good and evil, lest they die (vv. 16–17). But then the serpent beguiled the woman so that she desired this fruit and ate of it (Gen. 3:1–6). Genesis tells us, "She took of its fruit and ate, and she also gave some to her husband who was with her, and he ate" (Gen. 3:6). It was from the hand of his bride that Adam got the "apple"—with one bite already missing.

Notice here that Satan directed his first attack on God's creation via the man-woman relationship. Adam fell into sin by means of his allegiance to and love for his wife. This demonstrates not only how Satan can be immensely crafty in devising his temptations but, more importantly, how central marriage is to God's plan. Satan attacked at a point where the man and woman were vulnerable, but also because Satan saw the threat potential of their partnership. So where some may want to say, "See, I told you marriage is bad!" the truth is actually the opposite: marriage is so good that Satan attacked it first.

I believe that, faced with Satan's clever assault, Adam found himself in a quandary that became his undoing: He thought he must choose between the woman and God, between the gift (the woman) and the Giver. He seems to have thought that *refusing* the fruit meant a rejection of his wife in favor of God, and that *accepting* the fruit meant a rejection of God in favor of his wife. So great was Adam's devotion to the woman that he committed the grave sin of choosing her over God.

Adam's assessment of his dilemma was only half right. It was in fact a false dilemma, not at all the simple either/or choice he apparently perceived it to be. We do not know what would have become of Eve had Adam appealed to God for help in light of her sin. But we do know that joining Eve in rebellion against God's command was the wrong answer. God's gifts convey blessing only when enjoyed in obedience to God. By choosing to sin with Eve—choosing the gift over the Giver— Adam walked into Satan's clever trap and fell under God's condemnation. In the end, Adam fell not merely by choosing to sin but by preferring God's gift of his wife over God Himself.

This pattern shapes man's fallen attitude even today: sinful mankind desires the gifts and blessings of God but wants nothing to do with the One who provided them. We embrace the gift and reject the Giver. In no other area of life is this more true than in relations between the sexes. Unbelieving men desire to enjoy the blessings of female companionship on their own terms (typically with a focus on sex), taking God's gift as they think best for themselves. As a result, marriage and sexuality have become as much a curse in our society as a blessing.

This account from Genesis 3 is not a happy tale, and we

will be spending much of this chapter exploring the pernicious and relentless effects of sin in marriage that were unleashed that day in the garden. This is necessary, because if we are to learn to deal with sin effectively, we must face it clearly. But for those who need a glimmer of hope to sustain them through the next few pages, know that by the end of this chapter we will have identified and celebrated the solution to the problem that began in Genesis 3.

LOVE ESTRANGED

The aftermath of the first sin is just as instructive as the sin itself. The first thing we note is that sin immediately began ruining the relationship between the man and woman. "The eyes of both were opened, and they knew that they were naked" (Gen. 3:7). The free intimacy of their love relationship was polluted by sin and became "something unpleasant and filled with shame."[9] As a result, "they sewed fig leaves together and made themselves loincloths" (Gen. 3:7). This is how we live today. With our hearts and minds corrupted by sin, it is difficult to let anyone really know us, including (and sometimes especially) those closest to us. Moreover, our self-protective stratagems are often as pathetically ineffective as that of our first parents. No variation of hiding behind fig leaves can ever really make a difference. Only through the twin graces of forgiveness and repentance can Christians regain much of what was lost in sin, so that the unity God intends for marriage may be restored in significant degree.

More fundamental, however, than the alienation between man and woman is the alienation between God and man that results from sin. Adam and Eve "heard the sound of the Lord God walking in the garden in the cool of the day" (Gen. 3:8), so they hid among the trees. What could more perfectly describe the evil effects of sin than this flight from the presence of their good and loving God! When God challenged Adam for his behavior, our first father replied, "I was afraid, because I was naked, and I hid myself" (Gen. 3:10). "Who told you that you were naked?" God replied. "Have you eaten of the tree of which I commanded you not to eat?" (Gen. 3:11). Here we see the violent effects of sin, sundering the man not only from God but also from the woman: Adam answered, "The woman whom you gave to be with me, she gave me the fruit of the tree, and I ate" (Gen. 3:12). Adam thus became the first in a long line of male blame-shifters. As we put it today, he "threw Eve under the bus," betraying her in an effort to save his own skin. Before sin entered the garden, Adam was overwhelmed by the blessing of the woman (Gen. 2:23), but now he despised her and accused God for shackling him to her. Eve's defense was only slightly less ignoble, accepting no responsibility for her sin and blaming the serpent (and perhaps accusing God for his lack of protection): "The serpent deceived me, and I ate" (Gen. 3:13).

What a fine little mess sin made. Its power to do so being no less today, sin continues to sunder lives and marriages. Like Adam, men today find it easier to criticize and accuse our wives than to confess our sin. For some men, the conflict with their wives undermines their relationship with God. For others, their lack of a relationship with God leaves them unable to love their wives sacrificially.

MARRIAGE CURSED BY OUR FAILURE

If the situation was not already bad enough, God's response made things worse. In all of Genesis 2 and 3, I think nothing more accurately describes and explains the troubles we experience in marriage today than God's curses on the woman and man.

God's Curse on Woman

Perhaps because her sin was first, God began by addressing our first mother: "To the woman he said, 'I will surely multiply your pain in childbearing; in pain you shall bring forth children. Your desire shall be for your husband, and he shall rule over you'" (Gen. 3:16). If we consider how sin affects women in marriage today, in this two-part curse the arrow has pierced the very center of the target.

Pain. By this curse the act of childbirth, in so many ways the pinnacle of feminine experience, is made desperately painful and fearfully dangerous. Apart from this curse, pain would not be part of childbearing and delivery. It seems clear that a woman's monthly cycle—inextricably tied to the process of conception—would also be free of both pain and the hormonally induced mood swings that can wreak such havoc with women (and sometimes, by extension, their men).

Conflict. Even more directly targeting the marriage relationship is the second part of God's curse on the woman: "Your desire shall be for your husband, and he shall rule over you" (Gen. 3:16). Here is a cause for much of the struggle between the sexes. Notice that God curses the woman with an unwholesome desire toward the man. She was made as a helper for man (Gen. 2:18), but now that man-orientation is made a curse.

The word for *desire* that God employs here appears only two other times in the entire Bible. We read it in the Song of Solomon to describe a man's sexual craving: "I am my beloved's, and his desire is for me" (Song 7:10). God's curse applies this word to women, with the effect that they have an unhealthy infatuation with men and their relationships with them. The other occurrence appears in Genesis, where God warned Cain about the power of sin: "sin is crouching at the door. Its desire is for you" (Gen. 4:7). Here, the idea is mastery or control. Putting these two uses of the word together, we see that God has placed a curse on the woman so that she is gripped by an unwholesome desire to possess and control her man.

This, of course, is the actual experience of countless couples. Men often feel their wives are too controlling and too demanding in their relationship expectations. So men push back, just as God said: "and he shall rule over you." Remember, this is not just a problem that *some* women have. Rather, it is God's curse on women in general and on marriage. If you doubt this, I invite you to inspect the women's section of any magazine display or the checkout counter of any grocery store. What is the common thread of nearly every article in nearly every women's magazine? Whether the subject is sexual performance, dieting, cooking, or sewing, there is a focus on possessing and controlling a man. Underneath it all is the curse of God on our sinful mother: "Your desire shall be for your husband, and he shall rule over you" (Gen. 3:16). This curse is God's punishment for Adam and Eve's sin, magnifying the effects of sin on our relationships.

God's Curse on Man

To cut off any self-congratulatory snickering about the woman's sin, let us remember that immediately following the curse on the woman came the equally severe curse on the man.

> To Adam he said, "Because you have listened to the voice of your wife and have eaten of the tree of which I commanded you, 'You shall not eat of it,' cursed is the ground because of you; in pain you shall eat of it all the days of your life; thorns and thistles it shall bring forth for you; and you shall eat the plants of the field. By the sweat of your face you shall eat bread, till you return to the ground, for out of it you were taken; for you are dust, and to dust you shall return." (Gen. 3:17–19)

Because Adam was head of the first home, his sin had a broader effect than did his wife's sin, bringing God's curse on the very land Adam was supposed to work and keep. This should remind us that the primary threat to the safety of our loved ones is always our own sin. The arena where Adam was to bear God's image through labor was cursed, so that the earth could be made to bring forth food only with the greatest exertions, even as thorns and thistles grow on their own in lavish abundance. This is why my yard has its weed problem, why our work is so often a wearisome, life-sapping affair, and why death awaits us all at the end of our working days.

Notice how sin has had the effect of cursing the arrangements God had made in creation. This is what sin does—it doesn't make things different, it makes them painful. God made the man to direct himself outward toward the garden. With his wife lovingly at his side, he was to make things abundant and fruitful as he cultivated the ground and kept it safe. Now, the man's outward orientation is so demanding that he will show practically no attention to the woman at all. This is the very dynamic in virtually every marriage: the woman feels neglected because the man is consumed by his work, and if not his work, then his play: cars, music, sports, paintings, stamp collections, and whatnot. Isn't this what we find in every male-oriented magazine? Men's magazines are all about "stuff" outside our relationships: work, sports, politics, money, etc. Women, too, you say? Yes, but not women in actual relationships with men; instead, sinful man craves women merely as toys and possessions.

God's curse on the man draws him unwholesomely *away* from the woman, even as God's curse on the woman draws her unwholesomely *toward* the man. This is why most marital counseling sessions are some variation on this theme: Wife—"You don't pay any attention to me." Husband—"You are too demanding and nag too much." God has cursed the marriage relationship with a poisonous desire for control by the woman and a self-absorbed focus outside the relationship by the man.

THE PURPOSE OF THE CURSE

At this point, you may wonder: *Why would God do this? Wouldn't it have been better to strike Adam and his wife dead than to subject them to this torture?* But from the beginning, God had plans for our redemption, so even His curses are designed with redemption in view.

Remember how Adam accepted the apple from his wife, choosing the gift over the Giver as he ate the fruit from her hand? Through His curses, God rejected the very arrangement Adam was trying to establish: joy in marriage apart from submission to God's authority. His curses said, in effect, "You cannot enjoy marriage without returning your heart to me!" God's curses on the relationship were the poison for which God alone was the antidote. This is why marriage is practically hopeless apart from the grace of Christ, and why divorce is so rampant. The struggles that men and women experience in marriage are intended by God to drive us to our knees and to our Bibles, that we would restore God to the center of our lives.

The proof that God's curses were redemptive is found in the curses themselves—specifically one curse that preceded those given to the woman and man. After consigning the serpent to wriggling in the dirt all its life, God gave this curse to Satan: "I will put enmity between you and the woman, and between your offspring and her offspring; he shall bruise your head, and you shall bruise his heel" (Gen. 3:15).

The first part of this curse guaranteed that there would always be godly descendents of Adam and his wife standing in opposition to the ungodly descendents; Satan would never succeed at winning all of mankind to his unholy cause. But most significant here is God's promise regarding a particular seed of the woman: "He shall bruise your head, and you shall bruise his heel." Here is foretold the final defeat of Satan by the Lord Jesus Christ, who would be born of a woman and suffer the bruising of Satan's attacks as He hung on the cross. In the process, however, Jesus would crush Satan's head, destroying the foundation of Satan's kingdom by suffering the Father's wrath and dying to free us from our sins.

We also can see God's redemptive grace for the man and woman in the action He took just after pronouncing His curses: "The LORD God made for Adam and for his wife garments of skins and clothed them" (Gen. 3:21). God had said that if Adam sinned there would be death in the garden (Gen. 2:17), and now there was. But it was a substitute that paid the penalty for Adam's sin, as he and the woman were clothed in the hides of spotless, innocent animals. Here was foreshadowed the atoning work of Jesus, the Lamb who one day would die for our sins (John 1:29). Here also we see the imputation of Christ's righteousness—God clothing us in Christ's innocence—so that the man and woman, through faith in the promise of a Savior, might stand before God and receive His blessing. In fact, it was only after this that Adam decided what to call his wife, and I think it likely that the name he gave her was intended to express their shared faith in God's promise of a Messiah to come through her womb: "The man called his wife's name Eve, because she was the mother of all living" (Gen. 3:20).

OUR HOPE FOR RENEWAL

As we now prepare, at the end of this chapter and throughout the next, to consider New Testament teaching pertaining to marriage, let us revisit what we have learned from Genesis 2 and 3 on sin and redemption:

- There is a pattern to the effects of sin. Sin tends to alienate us from one another, just as it separates us from God. Sin brings guilt, and with guilt comes an inability to trust others or to allow them near.
- God's curse on the woman causes women to have an unhealthy desire to possess and even control men, the inevitable result of which is marital conflict. Men, called to work and keep the garden, find their work and play so absorbing that they have little attention to give to their wives.
- All this struggle within and among ourselves is intended by God to draw us back to Himself as we look to Jesus for forgiveness and righteousness. As we take off the fig leaves of our self-righteousness and cease shifting our blame onto others, instead confessing our sin and clothing ourselves with the righteousness of Christ, God will heal both us and our closest and most important human relationship, our marriage relationship with a woman.

So if the beginning of the story is genuinely tragic and destructive, the end is genuinely joyful and redemptive. I think the apostle Paul may have best summarized our hope for renewal and restoration as Christians. He wrote in Colossians of the blessings God has granted us in Jesus Christ, referring to us as "God's chosen ones, holy and beloved," and forgiven of our sins by the Lord (Col. 3:12–13).

These are the resources of grace that God has given to us: He chose us in Christ for salvation, He set us apart for salvation and new life, and He put his Fatherly love on us as dear children. In light of God's restored blessing for us in Jesus Christ, Paul sees us finally able to restore our relationship with other Christians, especially laying out the response of grace that we can now extend to our wives: "Put on then, as God's chosen ones, holy and beloved, compassion, kindness, humility, meekness, and patience" (Col. 3:12). These are the very things that sin tries to prevent me from offering—remember how sin caused Adam to condemn his wife in order to cover his own sin? But now, forgiven and sanctified by God in Christ, a Christian man is able to have compassion, kindness, humility, meekness, and patience toward his wife (and vice versa).

What a difference this makes. Paul continues, "bearing with one another and . . . forgiving each other" (Col. 3:13). Conscious of having been so wonderfully forgiven through Christ's blood, I now have the ability to forgive others who sin or let me down, just as my wife now has forgiving grace for me. "And above all these put on love, which binds everything together in perfect harmony. And let the peace of Christ rule in your hearts, to which indeed you were called in one body. And be thankful. Let the word of Christ dwell in you richly" (Col. 3:14–16).

Do you see how the curse of sin is redeemed in Christ? These verses are not meant merely to provide sentimental warmth to wedding napkins and wall hangings. Rather, they are the tangible agenda of God's restoring grace. I do not have to wait until I fully understand my wife in order to love her. In Christ, I have no warrant to withhold my love until she changes according to my self-serving agenda. I am free in Christ, through the resources of God's redeeming grace for me, to love my wife. Because God has forgiven me, I can truly forgive her. Because God has given to me, I can gladly give to her. With God's compassion for me, I have compassion to give; with God's grace I can show grace. And with God's Word dwelling in our relationship, my wife and I can grow in this grace so that we learn more and more to love one another while drawing more and more from the wells of God's saving love for us.

As I said in the previous chapter, knowing makes all the difference. It helps greatly to know what has gone wrong with mankind, and with men and women in particular. But it helps much more to know the grace that God has for us through faith in Jesus, the Lamb who takes away our sin. God wants us to know His worth as the Giver, so that He is at the center of all our worship and life. When we return to Him through faith in Christ and place Him at the center of our lives and marriages, God has abundant grace for us to give to others as God has given to us.

Questions for Reflection and Discussion

- How do you experience the pattern by which sinful man wants to enjoy God's gifts but reject God the Giver? Why is this a problem?

- Do you think it is fair to say that women tend to want to possess and control men? How does the curse on Eve describe this tendency? How does this desire lead to marital conflict? Is it likewise fair to say that men tend to be preoccupied outside the relationship? What is the problem with this pattern?

- How does the promise of the gospel—specifically as centered on God's depiction of an atoning sacrifice and imputed righteousness (the covering of Adam and Eve by the hides of innocent animals)—serve as the starting point for redeeming our marriages?

- What are the "resources of grace" laid out by Paul in Colossians 3:12–13? How do these serve as resources that enable us to respond differently and more lovingly to our wives?

Chapter 8

MARRIAGE AND THE MASCULINE MANDATE

One of the most important principles of Christian salvation is that redemption remedies the fall. The Bible depicts human history in terms of creation, fall, and redemption, the point of redemption being to secure God's purposes in creation and advance them to the conclusion He intended all along.

That redemption remedies the fall is very good news for us, because it means God has provided a solution to our biggest problems. Take death, for instance, which is the prime curse that resulted from sin. Because of Christ's resurrection, Christians may know with certainty that death will be defeated in our own resurrection at the end of the age. For guilt, Christ provides forgiveness. For sin's temptation, He provides the grace of His Holy Spirit. On it goes, through every category of life. Christian salvation is truly great! God in His goodness has not only withheld the punishment our sin deserves, but

His saving plan brings about all the blessings He originally intended, so that His people might know His love and bear His image in glory.

As we have been learning, this great salvation has everything to do with marriage. In Chapter 6, we considered marriage as God made it. In Chapter 7, we viewed marriage as sin marred it. Can we ever get back to the glories of the garden? The answer is not only "Yes," but because this is God's intention, we can be certain he will bring it to pass. His redemptive plan will advance us from this fallen creation all the way to the limitless and eternal glory He has prepared for us in the end. Christians therefore can be confident in God's redemption, even as we are realists in facing the troubles of sin. There may be no other relationship where this blend of confidence and realism is more warranted than Christian marriage.

Our study of Genesis 2:15 disclosed the twofold Masculine Mandate, based on God's original reason for placing man in the garden: "The LORD God took the man and put him in the garden of Eden to work it and keep it" (Gen. 2:15). Just as this mandate has been marred by sin, God's redeeming work in Christ restores men to our high calling and equips us to fulfill it. To revisit some of what we learned in Chapter 2, the term *work* signifies God's broad mandate for a nurturing and cultivating masculinity, which causes people and things to grow and become strong. The second term, *keep*, refers to man as a watchman and defender, keeping safe those under our care. By diligently observing the work-and-keep mandate, men fulfill their calling by building up and keeping safe.

New Testament teaching about marriage reveals that working and keeping is the very pattern of God's calling to a Christian husband. In this chapter, we will focus on the two main portions of the New Testament that outline a man's duty to his wife—Ephesians 5:22–33 and 1 Peter 3:7—fleshing out the details of these passages in terms of the man's mandate to work and keep.

MASCULINE HEADSHIP AND FEMININE SUBMISSION

Paul addresses the topic of marriage as part of his broader discussion of Christian conduct. His basic exhortation is for believers to be "imitators of God, as beloved children" (Eph. 5:1). Children learn by doing what their parents do, and we as God's children are to imitate Him. Paul expounds on this theme under the headings of moral purity (Eph. 5:3–20) and a Christian's calling to peaceable submission (Eph. 5:21–6:9). The apostle applies the calling to submission in a number of contexts: wives submitting to husbands (Eph. 5:22–33), children submitting to parents (Eph. 6:1–4), and slaves submitting to masters (Eph. 6:5–9). Paul is not saying that wives are like children or slaves, but rather that these are three kinds of relationships in which Christians are called to submit peaceably to divinely ordained authority. In these same passages, Paul addresses those in authority, exhorting them to use their power in ways that build up and protect.

When Paul addresses a husband in his duties to his wife, he clearly operates from the premise that the man has been given authority by God to lead in the home. First, he calls wives to submit to their own husbands out of reverence for Christ. "For the husband is the head of the wife even as Christ is the head of the church, his body, and is himself its Savior" (Eph. 5:23). After the brief exhortation to women, Paul launches a longer and more detailed teaching on the duties of the man:

> Husbands, love your wives, as Christ loved the church and gave himself up for her, that he might sanctify her, having cleansed her by the washing of water with the word, so that he might present the church to himself in splendor, without spot or wrinkle or any such thing, that she might be holy and without blemish. In the same way husbands should love their wives as their own bodies. He who loves his wife loves himself. For no one ever hated his own flesh, but nourishes and cherishes it, just as Christ does the church, because we are members of his body. (Eph. 5:25–30)

When we consider the Bible's command for our wives to submit to us, and how this is a remedy for their sinful tendency to show disrespect and challenge us for control, we can be tempted to adopt a condescending attitude. But as we see in this passage, how much worse is *our* situation! We have to be commanded by the Lord simply to love our wives!

When God gift-wrapped the first woman and placed her into Adam's arms, he shouted for joy. How much has changed since then. Sin has caused men to neglect the greatest gift—short of the saving work of Christ—that God has ever given us. When Paul writes the simple command, "Husbands love your wives," he lays bare the shameful heart of the problem with most married men.

Of course, Paul's purpose in writing was not primarily to condemn men but to encourage us in our Christian calling. If men wonder (and we do), "OK, *how* am I supposed to love my wife?" Paul answers in these verses. For starters, a husband loves his wife by leading the marriage and the home.

The husband is given headship by God. This is in part because God did not design wives to lead husbands (see also 1 Cor. 11:3). As we discussed in the previous chapter, God's curse upon women inclines them to frustration and futility as they crave a leadership they were neither designed to assume nor equipped to perform. Moreover, God's curses on man and woman have the effect of making everything we attempt more difficult. So despite this curse-based tendency in women to want to lead their husbands, most wives will nevertheless suffer anxiety if they *get* what they want, should their husbands' neglect force them to lead the home. What tragic ironies resulted from Adam and Eve's fall and God's subsequent curses.

To be clear, male leadership in marriage does not mean the husband does everything or even that he decides everything. Rather, it means he typically initiates and always leads those shared discussions with his wife by which the various aspects of marriage and family life are decided and planned. The wife's opinion is vitally important, and a godly couple should be a close-knit team. But there should be no area of family life in which the husband does not serve as leader, facilitator, and overseer. This is especially true when it comes to the family's commitment to godly principles and behaviors. A Christian wife should be able to look to her husband with respect, seeing a servant of Christ committed to the Lord's will being done in the home. A husband who seeks to practice headship in a context of partnership—fully respecting and encouraging his wife's contributions—is off to a good start on loving his wife.

TO WORK: A HUSBAND'S MINISTRY OF NURTURE

A husband's call with respect to his wife can be understood in terms of the original mandate God gave to men—to work and keep. Paul's teaching on marriage emphasizes the alignment of a husband's ministry to that of Christ's for the church. Wives should submit to their husbands because the husband is given a limited but genuinely Christlike role in the marriage. That is, just as Christ builds up His people, so a Christian husband is to edify and encourage his wife. This is the "work" component of a husband's role—his calling to maintain a nurturing ministry of love toward his wife.

We see this call in Paul's statement that Christ labored to "sanctify" the church, "having cleansed her by the washing of water with the word" (Eph. 5:26). To sanctify is to "make holy." Paul then explains that Christ wanted to present the church to himself "in splendor, without spot or wrinkle or any such thing, that she might be holy and without blemish" (Eph. 5:27). This tells us that a husband's first concern for his wife should be her spiritual well-being: her relationship to the Lord and the strength and power of her faith. Paul is not saying that husbands should violently press their wives into some idea of how a Christian wife should act. Rather, husbands should look on their Christian wives as holy in God's sight, and should treat them, in Peter's words, as "heirs with [them] of the grace of life" (1 Peter 3:7).

In short, a husband is called to build up his wife's faith and hope in Christ through his ministry of God's Word in her life. Paul says that Jesus "cleansed" the church—His people—"by the washing of water with the word" (Eph. 5:26). This may seem confusing, since Jesus cleansed us with His atoning blood. But Paul is referring here to the way that Jesus called for His gospel message to be preached, so that through faith in Him people might be cleansed and forgiven. Likewise, Paul says, a Christian husband is to minister the gospel promises of the Bible to the encouragement of his wife.

Paul's teaching on marriage is complemented by a parallel passage from Peter, a passage that, if anything, is even more clear and direct. After commanding wives to submit to their husbands, Peter turns to the men: "Likewise, husbands, live with your wives in an understanding way, showing honor to the woman as the weaker vessel, since they are heirs with you of the grace of life, so that your prayers may not be hindered" (1 Peter 3:7).

Peter answers a question we all ought to ask when faced with Paul's teaching about a husband's ministry of God's Word: "What am I supposed to say to her? How am I supposed to know what will encourage my wife from Scripture?" Peter answers in three ways. First, he says, live in close communion with your wife. Second, pay attention to her and get to know what is going on inside her. Third, he insists, act in a way that says you cherish her deeply. Let's consider each of these important commands for husbands.[10]

Live Together

First, Peter says, "husbands, live with your wives." Most men respond, "All right, I can check that one off. We live in the same house!" But, of course, that's not Peter's point. Rather, you are to live *with* your wife. The word for "live with" is the Greek word that means "commune" and gives us the noun *community*. Peter is saying that husbands are to live with their wives in a single shared life.

Husbands are to take an interest in the things the wife is interested in (the wife is to do likewise). The couple is to spend time together and to live in one rhythm. With this in mind, I find it important that as much as possible a husband and wife go to bed together and rise together. It is extremely valuable for a couple to talk and pray in the evening before falling to sleep, and to start the day with encouragement and prayer. Peter is clearly suggesting that a husband who lives in communion with his wife will be better able to minister to her.

Pay Attention

Elaborating his point, the apostle says men should live with their wives "in an understanding way." This passage contains one of my main Bible-translation points of frustration. The original text does not say men are merely to "be understanding" or, as the New International Version puts it, to live "with consideration." Peter is not merely telling husbands to put the toilet seat down (although that is not a bad idea). The Greek text actually says that husbands must live with their wives "according to knowledge." In other words, a husband must know what is going on with his wife.

Here's a quiz I give to husbands who desire to be more faithful in ministry to their wives. If I stop you at any time, will you be able to give me a rough sketch of your wife's schedule for that day? Can you identify at least one major issue that is on her mind and weighing down her heart, making her afraid or frustrated or concerned? These are the things Peter has in mind. Most husbands have not the slightest clue what is going on with their wives' schedules, much less what challenges are weighing on their hearts. One good way to find out is to ask. A husband might say, "Honey, I want to minister to you today, so can you tell me if anything is burdening your heart?" Now, if he has been communing with her, as the verse said earlier, he probably won't even have to ask. But when in doubt, he should certainly ask. The reality is that a husband must know what is going on in the heart and mind of his wife if he is to minister to her faithfully in prayer and with God's Word.

Show Honor

Peter also tells husbands to live "showing honor to the woman" (1 Peter 3:7). The point here is not merely that a husband should be courteous and polite to his wife, although this is certainly good counsel. The word for "showing honor" might be better rendered as "cherishing" her (the Greek word here, *time'*, is used for assigning a high price to objects in the market). A husband is to convey to his wife that he values her greatly, that she is precious to him. Is the best way to do this through gifts of flowers or jewelry? My experience says that these are relatively easy ways of communicating a wife's preciousness. I think the main way is through Peter's first two commands: our time and attention. I would recommend that a husband simply ask his wife, "What makes you feel that I value you?" and take seriously what she has to say.

In Sum, Nourish and Cherish

Combining the counsel of Peter and Paul, we see that a husband committed to nurturing his wife will do more than just try to make her feel good. He will get involved and remain involved in her life. He will pay attention to her and share his life with her. Then, out of the far more intimate and comprehensive knowledge he now has of his wife, he will minister God's Word to known areas of burden, fear, or doubt, so as to build up her faith and her identity in Christ.

Christ labored to make His church holy, Paul says, by cleansing her with the Word. "In the same way," he urges, "husbands should love their wives as their own bodies. He who loves his wife loves himself" (Eph. 5:28). This makes Peter's point that a husband has to be close to his wife and know her like he knows his own body. Paul says that the two really are that close in the marital bond. "For no one ever hated his own flesh, but nourishes and cherishes it, just as Christ does the church" (Eph. 5:29).

Notice the combination of "nourish" and "cherish." We nourish our wives with God's Word by cherishing them so as to be close to their hearts. So when a husband knows his wife is weighed down under the burdens of child-raising, he might say to her, "[cast] all your anxieties on him, because he cares for you" (1 Peter 5:7). A husband who knows his wife feels unlovely or depressed can minister the balm of God's Word to the bruised spot in her heart: "The LORD your God is in your midst, a mighty one who will save; he will rejoice over you with gladness; he will quiet you by his love; he will exult over you with loud singing" (Zeph. 3:17). A husband who knows his wife is grieving a loss might encourage her to take her heart to the Lord: "The LORD is near to the brokenhearted and saves the crushed in spirit" (Ps. 34:18). The point is not that a husband is to drop stock Bible lines onto his wife's head, but that he is sensitively and caringly seeking to apply God's Word to encourage, strengthen, instruct, and exhort her in the truth and grace of the Lord.

Many husbands will reply, "I'm not sure I know the Bible well enough to minister to my wife's needs in that way." That is precisely God's point: in obedience to Him, God wants us to be motivated by our love for our wives and their need of our ministry to become the men of faith and biblical knowledge we are intended to be.

For our marriages to regain the love and unity God designed them to have, it is not merely a matter of wives submitting to their husbands in the Lord. Husbands, in fact, have the first and greatest responsibility. As we gain insight about our wives through our shared lives together and our attentive and cherishing interest in the affairs of their hearts, we must nourish our wives with God's Word, and with our own encouraging and upbuilding words informed by Scripture. This is the essential "to work" teaching of Peter and Paul to husbands.

TO KEEP: DYING FOR HER TO LIVE

Along with a husband's nurturing ministry to his wife is his guardian protection to ensure she is safe. This is the "to keep" mandate by which a husband guards and protects his wife. Paul could hardly express this in more vivid language than when he compares a husband's self-sacrificing love to the cross-bearing love of Jesus Christ: "Husbands, love your wives, as Christ loved the church and gave himself up for her" (Eph. 5:25). As I noted earlier, the sacrificial work of Christ on the cross is the ultimate act of "keeping," safeguarding the blessings of God and conquering the enemies of sin and death.

Safe Even from You

When Paul says that a husband must embrace self-sacrifice for the sake of his wife's well-being, this of course includes her physical safety. But the main threat against which a man must protect his wife is *his own sin*. A friend once expressed his awakening to this truth in these words: "I used to think that if a man came into my house to attack my wife, I would certainly stand up to him. But then I came to realize that the man who enters my house and assaults my wife every day is me, through my anger, my harsh words, my complaints, and my indifference. As a Christian, I came to realize that the man I needed to kill in order to protect my wife is myself as a sinner." This is exactly right.

Peter gets at this role of heart-protector by saying that we show "honor to the woman as the weaker vessel." I earlier said that the word *honor* means to "cherish" the woman. When a man cherishes a woman, he not only nurtures her but also protects her so she feels safe from verbal abuse, ridicule, and scorn—especially his own—for these are darts that pierce her tender heart.

As a Man under Authority

Peter also reminds husbands that they are neither the ultimate authority over their wives nor the only one committed to her protection. A Christian wife happens to be a daughter of the Lord. Therefore, Peter warns husbands to give "honor to the woman as the weaker vessel, since they are heirs with you of the grace of life, so that your prayers may not be hindered" (1 Peter 3:7).

I have had many men ask me, "Does this verse really mean that if I do not love my wife as God wants me to, it will negatively affect God's relationship with me?" The answer is obvious: "You bet it does." That is the plain meaning of the words, isn't it? God is saying to husbands, who receive the privileges of covenant headship but also the obligations: "Don't think your relationship with Me is unaffected by your relationship with that dear woman, My daughter, whom I have given you in marriage. If you are going to neglect your covenant obligations to her, do not come into My presence claiming My covenant obligations to you."

I am not suggesting for a moment that a man's salvation is achieved by loving his wife or that a man who neglects his wife will necessarily be forsaken by God. But this verse clearly indicates that our day-to-day relationship with the Lord, and thus our own spiritual well-being, is directly related to our covenant faithfulness in nurturing and protecting our wives—who are, after all, the heavenly Father's little girls.

God placed us in the garden of marriage "to work it and keep it." The Lord is generous to us and abounds with mercy and grace for His sons. But He demands that we fulfill our ministry obligations to our wives.

A CHRISTLIKE REDEEMER

For a biblical example of how a husband may love his wife by nurturing and protecting her, we can look to Boaz in his care for Ruth—even before they were married. Ruth was an extremely vulnerable woman, being a foreigner from the hated land of Moab, and a widow with no male headship to protect her. She had returned to Bethlehem with her Jewish mother-in-law, Naomi, who also had lost everything with the death of her husband. Desperate to survive, Ruth went into the fields with poor Israelite women to glean grain that was left after the harvest. It happened that she came to the fields of Boaz, who approached her and said this:

"Now, listen, my daughter, do not go to glean in another field or leave this one, but keep close to my young women. Let your eyes be on the field that they are reaping, and go after them. Have I not charged the young men not to touch you? And when you are thirsty, go to the vessels and drink what the young men have drawn." (Ruth 2:8–10)

Ruth had caught Boaz's eye so that he treated her as a godly man should treat a Christian woman: he nurtured her and took steps for her protection. Ruth wondered at this treatment, and Boaz explained:

"All that you have done for your mother-in-law since the death of your husband has been fully told to me, and how you left your father and mother and your native land and came to a people that you did not know before. The LORD repay you for what you have done, and a full reward be given you by the LORD, the God of Israel, under whose wings you have come to take refuge!" (Ruth 2:11–12)

These are words to bless any woman's heart, and a model for how men should speak to build up their wives. Boaz did not merely appreciate her womanly form, but also the faith and virtue in her heart. So he invited Ruth to participate in the harvesters' meals, and he rather obviously arranged for his workers to leave a good bit of grain behind where Ruth was gleaning, as well as watch over her safety. Given Boaz's care and protection of Ruth, it is not in the least surprising that she gave her heart to him. This is how a husband loves his wife. He does what makes her feel loved, and she responds to him with love in return.

Later, at the harvest festival, Ruth's mother-in-law, Naomi, coached her as to what she should do. After Boaz had attended the feast and gone to lie down on a bale of grain, Ruth "came softly and uncovered his feet and lay down." When Boaz awoke, he discovered her lying at his feet. "Who are you?" he asked. She answered, "I am Ruth, your servant. Spread your wings over your servant, for you are a redeemer" (Ruth 3:7–9). We should not read anything sexual into this action. Rather, it is a vivid depiction of the love of a godly man for a woman finding its response in the giving of her heart. Ruth was placing herself under Boaz's authority and offering him her love. "Spread your wings over me," she said, beautifully expressing a woman's desire for provision and protection from a man. And note her attraction for him: "for you are a redeemer."

It is not too much to understand Ruth as saying here to Boaz, "You are like Christ to me." Not "you are Christ," but "you are *like* Christ." This is precisely how a wife should relate to her husband: "For the husband is the head of the wife even as Christ is the head of the church, his body, and is himself its Savior" (Eph. 5:23). She is to see her husband as a man who sacrifices himself so that she may live—so that her heart may be kept safe and flourish with grace under his loving care. A wife is the garden a godly husband "works and keeps," and her growth in spiritual beauty should be among his chief delights.

ASSURANCE OF BLESSING

In the next chapter, we will look at the ministry of men as fathers to their children. But we should conclude our studies on marriage by noting the strong synergies between being a Christlike husband and being a godly father.

There may be nothing more powerful in the lives of children than for their parents to enjoy a godly, grace-filled marriage. What a blessing it is for boys and girls to grow up with their mothers respecting their fathers, and their fathers ministering to their mothers with nurture and protecting care. But there is one other blessing in all this. Through our obedience to God's Word, we can be confident of His blessing on our families.

So it was for Boaz and Ruth after their wedding. The book of Ruth ends with a brief summary of their family tree. Their son was named Obed, who "was the father of Jesse, the father of David" (Ruth 4:17). Through the children of Boaz and Ruth would come the king for God's people, and through his line the Son of God would be born.

How wonderful that a man's godly love for his wife, in accordance with God's Word and performed on God's behalf, receives God's blessing so as to leave a mighty spiritual legacy (independent of whether they have children, by the way). For Boaz and Ruth, it started in the grain fields where Boaz spied her and offered biblical, manly love. It can start in our households today if we as men are willing to come before the Lord and seek His grace to begin loving our wives and providing the redeeming grace of Christ to our homes. We are no substitutes for Jesus, nor can we ever be. But our wives, receiving Christ-like love from us, should be able to say what Ruth answered to Boaz: "Spread your wings over me. For you are a redeemer."

Questions for Reflection and Discussion

- Why is it so important that the husband lead the marriage and the home? What happens to a wife when her husband won't lead? What happens to a man when he is not leading his home?

- Why are a husband's encouraging words so important to a wife? What is it in a woman's make-up that makes her husband's attention and nurturing care so important to her? What behaviors on your part would your wife say make her feel cherished? Is there a reason why you cannot do these things regularly?

- What types of sins in husbands tend to make wives feel unsafe? Which of your sins do you need to die to for the sake of your wife?

- What do you think of Ruth's statement to Boaz: "You are a redeemer"? In what ways is this description appropriate for any Christian husband? How can you best represent Christ as the head of your home and marriage?

Chapter 9

TO WORK:
THE DISCIPLING
OF CHILDREN

One lament common to Christian fathers goes something like this: "Pastor, I don't know how this happened. He has gone to church his whole life. We have taken him to Sunday school and Vacation Bible School, and paid for Christian school tuition. We have monitored his friends to make sure they come from good families, and we spanked him when he was little. I thought those things would keep this from happening!"

The child in this all-too-familiar story, who may be male or female, may have gotten involved in drugs, gotten pregnant, or rejected the faith. The father's underlying assumption is that providing a Christian structure for children is sufficient to ensure their godliness. If we can just control their school, their church, their books, their friends, their television diet, and their computer use, we think we can guarantee a comprehensive Christian faithfulness.

This belief is false. To follow it is a recipe for potential disaster.

FATHERS AND THE MASCULINE MANDATE

As I hope is clear by now, the main premise of this book is that the mandate of Genesis 2:15 summarizes our calling as men in our various roles. God put Adam in the garden "to work it and keep it," and the only difference between Adam's calling and ours lies in the details of how we seek to fulfill it.

So far, I have laid the doctrinal groundwork for this position and developed the theme within marriage, where a woman is to be built up and kept safe by her husband. But does this mandate apply to a man's calling as father? It absolutely does. In fact, according to the Bible, the two main obligations of fatherhood are to nurture (work) and protect (keep). A man is called to work the hearts of his children that they might become fertile soil for the gospel and devotion to Christ. And a man is called to keep and protect his children from the influences of sin—in the world and in their own hearts—so that all the efforts to draw that young person's heart to Christ may not be swept away.

It is good—and, yes, even necessary—for Christian parents to provide a solid and wholesome spiritual structure for their children. But there is no substitute for parents, on the one hand, personally discipling their children in the Lord and, on the other hand, disciplining them as necessary. Note the difference in spelling: *discipline* (covered in the next chapter) is essential as an act of keeping. But it cannot take the place of *discipling*, an act of working, the process of bonding with our children so as to guide their hearts personally to faith in Jesus.

"GIVE ME YOUR HEART"

If I had to pick just one verse on parenting from the book of Proverbs—the main source of our biblical wisdom on this subject—it would be Proverbs 23:26. Here we have the very pulse of the Bible's teaching on a father's relationship with his children, including God the Father's relationship with us, His sons in Christ. This verse provides the perspective behind all the wisdom passed from father to son in the Proverbs. In it, the father simply pleads, "My son, give me your heart." This is the prime aspiration of a true father toward his children. All the advice and commands found in Proverbs flow from this great passion: the desire of a loving father for the heart of his child, and for that child's heart to be given to the Lord.

The heart, of course, is the key to everything. "Keep your heart with all vigilance," we read, "for from it flow the springs of life" (Prov. 4:23). Biblically, the heart is the entire inner person, including the thoughts, desires, affections, and will. The heart is who we are inside—the real, essential person; the person God wants to own completely. A wise father wants to reach his child's heart, aiming for the willing offering of that heart both to himself as earthly father and to God as heavenly Father.

Note carefully that the proverb does not say, "My son, give me your behavior." It is not difficult for us to use our authority so that our children obey us outwardly without giving us their hearts. In fact, this lowest-common-denominator form of fatherly leadership is exactly what we will fall into if we don't actively seek a different and better result.

Neither does the proverb say, "My son, give me your physical presence," as if all that matters is placing a child in the right places at the right times. Worship, for instance, is far more than being physically present at church on Sunday morning, although many parents content themselves with little more from their children.

This, then, is the purpose of parental discipling: ministering to our children's hearts so as to gain a relationship of love with them and a shared heart-bond of faith in Jesus Christ. A father can spend years giving his child a Christian structure of church, Sunday school, Christian schooling, etc. If he then finds himself helpless as his young-adult child embraces rebellion, what has gone wrong? Too often the answer is that he never aimed for the child's heart and, not aiming for it, never gained it.

So the great issue of parental discipleship is directing the hearts of our children to the Lord. Instead of a mere focus on behavior or bodily presence, wise and loving parents seek to touch and win the hearts of their boys and girls.

The question is, how? First, understand that the heart—even the heart of a child—can only be given freely; it can never really be taken. In part, therefore, this is a matter of a father leading by example. We must begin by giving to our children what we seek to receive from them. Before we can convincingly plead, "My child, give me your heart," it must be evident to the child we have sincerely given our own.

Give Them Your Heart

Such a giving of a father's heart to a child is not a one-time event but a continual demonstration of love, patience, grace, mercy, and dedication over time. Our children must gain from us what they most desire: our affection, our approval, our attention, our involvement, and our time. Generally this will require us to resist the draw of other passions. Just as we have limited time and limited energy, we have limited love and a limited sphere of things to which we can give our hearts. Just as many mothers must lay aside other passions and preferences to serve their husbands and children, most fathers will have to curb or set aside career ambitions, recreational pastimes that do not involve their children, and indeed much of their lives apart from their families. This is what it takes to have the time and passion available to give our hearts to our children (and to our wives).

I think about this a lot because I am the kind of zealous person who does things like write this book. I pastor an active congregation and travel a bit to preach. This is all fine, so long as it does not keep me from giving my heart to my wife and children.

Is it possible for a father to lead an active, zealous, and productive work life while maintaining strong, heart-based relationships with his children? The answer is "Yes." It all depends on the father's heart. Is he connected with what is going on inside his son or daughter? Does he show interest and does he make time to let his children tell their endless stories about what they have been doing? If a father sincerely practices the four steps that I set out later in this chapter—Read, Pray, Work, Play—I believe he will be able to lead a very active work life without hindering his relationship with his children. But if the father frequently says, "I'm sorry, I don't have time," the child will inevitably point his heart elsewhere—someplace there is interest, attention, and excitement about his or her life. It is precisely a child's deep need for a sense of belonging that explains many of the troubles of young people—everything from drugs and gangs to premature romantic entanglements.

One Father's Example

The year 1972 was big for me, for two reasons. That year I turned 12 and entered sixth grade. More importantly, though, my father spent the entire year in Vietnam. He had often been away for maneuvers or short deployments of up to a month or so. He had even done an earlier long tour in Vietnam, although I was much younger then and hadn't noticed his absence too deeply. But this time, my dad would be at war for one of my most formative years.

What a hole my father's absence left in my life and the life of my mother and brother. I have many sad memories from that year. We lived in constant fear for my father's life, a fear made far more real by the fact that numerous friends' fathers had already died in Vietnam.

But not all the memories are sad. One of the most powerful memories is the thrill of the letter I would receive from my father almost every week. He and my mother wrote mostly every day, and our family would make a cassette recording to send to Dad every weekend. (What a difference the Internet must make for war families today!)

Recalling my personal letters from Dad practically brings me to tears even now. He would begin simply by telling me about his life. Not big military issues, but "neat stuff" that happened or that he saw. Then he would talk to me about my life, writing things like this:

Dear Ricky,
... I heard you had a great baseball game and made a great catch. Your mother told me how exciting it was when you won. How I wish I could have been there, but I can see you making that catch in my mind. ...

Do you see what he was doing? My dad was telling me that I was his boy and that his heart was fully engaged with me, even from halfway around the world. I knew he meant it because those letters merely carried on the same close relationship we had shared before he deployed. But make no mistake—there were rebukes, too, for I was a 12-year-old boy temporarily without a father in the home:

Dear Ricky,
... I was very displeased to hear that you have been talking back to your mother lately. You know that while I am serving our country, I count on you to be an obedient son. ...

My father's letters discussed everything in my life: school, church, sports, and home life, the details having been faithfully related to him by my mother. In the midst of a life-and-death war zone, with all the weighty responsibilities of a senior Army officer, my father was truly absorbed in my life. And I knew it. So when he said to me, in effect, "My son, give me your heart," he had already given every bit of his heart to me, his boy. I couldn't possibly help giving my heart back to him.

I was close to my father until the day he entered heaven. I had the privilege of being at his side reading psalms aloud to him as he departed from this life. When he was buried at Arlington National Cemetery, my brother and I gave a eulogy explaining what a privilege and blessing it had been to be the son of this fine man. I will never forget meeting with many of his old Army friends afterward. One of them, a general I had known well while growing up, looked me in the eye and said, "I would give anything to have my son speak at my funeral the way you spoke about Dave today." I didn't have the heart to respond honestly, because I knew him and I knew his son. His child would never speak about him the way I had spoken of Dad, because he had not given his heart to his son, and his son's heart was bitterly estranged from him. There was no point in me telling the general this, but I pray I never forget it when it comes to my own children.

FOUR WAYS TO REACH A CHILD'S HEART

Of course, not just any fatherly involvement can reach the hearts of our children. To really open up a child's heart, a father must observe the work-and-keep model of Genesis 2:15. There must be the working—as a father nurtures and cultivates the soil of a child's heart. And there must be the keeping—the correction that, as we will see in the following chapter, is to be exercised in a relationship of joy and love.

I am constantly amazed at the number of people who assure me that their fathers hardly ever praised them, but constantly criticized and berated. I meet people all the time who tell me that their fathers beat into their heads that they were losers who would never succeed. I can scarcely imagine what that is like. There is only so much a pastor can do to remedy such an upbringing, and the best he can do will include pointing such a person to the effective healing love of our heavenly Father, who can do far more than any man. But as fathers we can ensure that our own children are raised with the rich fertilizer of fatherly affection and esteem.

A godly father plants good things in the hearts of his children. He plants:

- The seeds of his own faith in Christ.
- A longing for truth and goodness.
- His hopes and dreams for the godly man or woman the child will become.
- His own confidence that the child has all the gifting and capacity needed to serve God faithfully in whatever way God may genuinely call.

A godly father works these things into the soil of his child's heart as he shares his own heart, listens to and molds the child's heart, and waters these tender plants with faith and love.

At the core of godly fatherhood is exactly this kind of emphasis on sharing his own heart and developing his child's heart. What can we do to forge such a parent-child bond? It is often observed, and rightly so, that *quality* time cannot substitute for *quantity* time. So what kinds of quantity time must fathers spend with their children?

I have an approach to this that involves four simple categories: Read, Pray, Work, Play. That is, I want to forge a relationship with each of my children as we read God's Word together, pray together, work together, and play together.

Read

First is the father's ministry of God's Word. There simply is no substitute for our children hearing the Word of God read from our lips, with its doctrines explained clearly so they can understand, and the message applied to their hearts. (This is not to denigrate a mother's equally important ministry of Scripture.)

It is not sufficient for fathers to send their children to church, Sunday school, Christian camp, or private Christian school. You must read the Bible to your children yourself. Obviously, our children must see some correspondence between the Bible and our lives. But even as we work out our own Christian growth, we must read God's Word to and with our children.

God's Word is "living and active" (Heb. 4:12). It gives life to believing hearts (Isa. 55:10–11) and imparts light to the eyes and wisdom to the inner man (Ps. 19:7–9). Holy Scripture should form a regular part of our conversation, so that families are not merely reading the Bible as some kind of ritual but studying and discussing together its life-giving teaching.

If we cannot make time to read the Bible together as a family, we should seriously reflect on our priorities. Most Christians today did not grow up in homes that practiced family devotions, but it is imperative that we revive this practice of family piety. We do not have to be elaborate, as if someone from church will be grading us. The family can simply gather for a reading of God's Word or a good devotional book with scriptural teaching, followed by discussion and prayer. (It is even better if the family can sing together.)

For some families, this time happens most naturally at breakfast, and in other families during or after dinner. A more prolonged gathering for family worship might occur once a week or so, but briefer devotions should occur more or less daily. The father does not have to be a Bible scholar, but he must read and teach Scripture to his children. As he does so in faith, God's Word will bind the hearts of fathers and children together in the unity of truth.

Pray

Another way men work the garden under their care is through a nurturing ministry of prayer. This is accomplished as parents bond with their children by praying for them and with them.

Prayer, like Scripture, is an absolutely nonnegotiable element of faithful parenting, one that communicates our sincere love to our children's hearts and shows them our reliance on the Lord's sovereign provision of grace. Our children need to grow up hearing their mother and father praying for them, and they need to have frequent experience praying with their parents. Naturally, much of this prayer will involve adoration of God and intercession for those outside the family. But parents should pray for the specific needs of their children—the things that, at that moment, are pressing on their hearts—and their children need to hear these heartfelt prayers. This means we have to know our kids, including the burdens they are facing—whether peer pressure, a health concern, anxiety over tests, or difficulties with friends.

One day my daughter and I were talking about a trial that was weighing greatly on her heart. She expressed her frustration not only with the situation but with God, crying out, "Daddy, I *know* you've been praying for me, so why doesn't God answer your prayers?" How encouraging that my daughter had noticed my prayer ministry for the affairs of her heart; this was a question I was happy to deal with.

We should also be open with our children about our need for *them* to pray for *us*. Sometimes these will involve adult issues, where children ought not to be concerned with the details. But they can know the basic issue, like this: "Daddy is facing difficult pastoral decisions, so we need to pray for God's wisdom and help for him." Or, "Daddy is dealing with a problem at work that requires God's guidance and direction." Any real relationship is two-way, and a close relationship with our children will involve our requests for them to pray for the real needs of our own lives.

Work

Third, if I want to draw close to my children, I need to work with them. By this I mean assisting them with whatever tasks and projects are before them.

When it comes to schoolwork, fathers must convey more than high expectations and demands. We must also be involved in our children's studies, helping them where they have problems and providing general support and encouragement.

Other areas of endeavor should also be of sincere interest and concern to fathers. To be genuine, we need to back up these expressed interests with concrete action. This may mean assembling invitations for a birthday party, contributing to a scrapbook, or helping a boy build arm strength because he'd like to try out as a Little League pitcher. The more we are involved in our children's work in a supportive, encouraging way, the more their lives will be intertwined with ours in a bond of love.

The relational two-way street applies here as well. As much as possible, we need to involve our children in our own work. This probably does not mean our 9-to-5 employment. But it does mean chores, yard work, and basic household maintenance. My children, especially the boys, love to help me work on things around the house. Since I am not particularly adept in this area, it challenges my patience to involve children who are even less competent. Taking the time to include and teach them makes everything slower and more difficult. But so what? Far more important than the pace of progress is the relationship with my children that is being strengthened as we work together.

Play

Lastly, fathers should play with and alongside their children. This involves stooping to their play and inviting them into ours. Simply put, families need to share fun, lighthearted times together.

This was harder when my children were very little, because I found it difficult to play with their small-child toys (this undoubtedly reveals a deficiency on my part). But as they have grown, I have found some of their toys a little more appealing. For the boys, this now means mostly Legos and the video games that are rationed to them. I need to know about and be "into" all the Lego vehicles they make (Star Wars ships, mainly), letting them explain to me all the details of their creations. I also need to know enough about their video games to be able to follow (more or less) their conversations on these subjects. Do I need to be constantly honing my video-game controller skills and gunning for the high score at whatever version of *Mario* has captured their attention? Of course not. But it is important for me to have some appreciation for these games my boys love, and make some time to play with them.

The same is true with daughters. Naturally, some girl play is not all that appealing to dads, but we must take an eager interest in what our daughters are doing and let them enjoy telling us about their dolls and play sets. This is how we become part of their world in a way that draws their hearts to us.

As children grow older, I firmly believe the whole family should play indoor games together and engage in outdoor recreation as a family. These playtimes create shared experiences that are interesting and fun, and bind our hearts together as a family.

Fathers also need to invite their children into their own games (which presupposes that we should not have interests that draw us into sin). For instance, I am a lifelong Boston Red Sox baseball fan, but I had quit following baseball for more than ten years, primarily due to a lack of time. When my boys reached elementary school, however, I revived my interest in the Red Sox so I could share it with my boys—the girls are now involved, too. This gives us something we share, and pretty much every summer evening we check the scoreboards to see how our team is doing. We follow the players we love and we ride the highs and lows of dedicated fans, experiencing all this together.

This is my simple agenda to ensure I am actively and intimately involved in the lives of my children: Read, Pray, Work, Play. I must read God's Word to and with my children regularly. We must bear each others' burdens in prayer and worship the Lord together at His throne of grace. My children need my positive, encouraging involvement in their work (and they need an invitation into some of mine). And we need to bind our hearts with laughter and joy in shared play, both one-on-one and as a complete family. This all requires time, for time is the currency with which I purchase the right to say, "My son, my daughter, give me your heart."

DIFFERENT SEASONS, ONE GOAL

When children are little, parents tell them what to do, and the children are called to obey. But as our children grow, our power over them increasingly consists of influence rather than authority. The progression through adolescence and young adulthood requires our children to take more and more responsibility for their actions, making choices and decisions according to what they think and desire, not what we tell them. Of course, this requires parents to change, too, as we gradually release our hold and transition from dictating to guiding—from the power of command to the influence of carefully timed and chosen counsel.

My point here is not merely to encourage parents of older children to be willing to let your children gradually make decisions independently (although if the shoe fits, you should wear it). Being aware of this transition is certainly important for the parents of older children. But this awareness is even more important for parents of younger children.

How vital yet fleeting is the season of parenting young children. I know it can seem sometimes as if those early years will go on forever, but they don't. In relatively short order your children will naturally begin to move beyond the influence of your authority, and this is exactly as it should be. The moment that happens—and it actually starts at a fairly young age—your opportunity to reach their hearts begins to decrease, slipping away gradually day by day.

It is in anticipation of this transition, therefore, that fathers must work for the close bond of a loving relationship all through the childhood years. The time to impress on a child the central importance of Scripture is not in high school, but in preschool. Likewise, time spent building goodwill and trust during a child's elementary school years may be vitally important during the years of immature young adulthood, when the minds of our kids can be clouded and bewildered by change.

Well do I remember the influence of my relationship with my parents during high school. Because of their investment in me all through my life, I was close to them. So, as a foolish young adult, my identification with their values and my desire not to let them down played a major role in directing and restraining my behavior. "My son, give me your heart," the wise man said. The child who has done this sincerely is one who trusts, admires, and loves his or her parents—and is therefore more likely to navigate the pressures and trials of adolescence in safety.

One day, your children will encounter outside the home temptations and spiritual attacks of substantial power. The toxic youth culture they will discover can threaten to overwhelm by sheer force almost any child's desire not to disappoint his or her parents. But we have a greater hope. A passion for the glory of Jesus and a living awareness of gospel realities will provide our children with both offensive and defensive capabilities they otherwise never would have possessed. This is why the greatest, most powerful, and most valuable passion a father can give his children is a passion for the Lord and His gospel of grace.

The ultimate reason we desire our children to give us their hearts is so that we can guide their hearts to Jesus. This is our aim in Bible reading, prayer, and family life together. The more we can convey our own wonder and joy in the Lord—the more our children can see the reality and power of God's grace expressed in our lives of compassion, joy, and holiness—the more attractive Jesus will be to our boys and girls. We must lead our children to the Lord so they have opportunity to hear Him say, "Come to me" (Matt. 11:28). We must let them see the light of Jesus in our lives, in our minds, and in the passion of our hearts. Because, as Jesus said, if our children will see Him as the light of the world and follow Him, "they will not walk in darkness, but will have the light of life" (John 8:12). That is our ultimate goal, and the greatest motivation for fathers to open their own hearts to the Lord, that Jesus might be made attractive and inviting through us.

Questions for Reflection and Discussion

- What is the difference between discipling and discipline? How are they related? Why are both absolutely needed in the Christian upbringing of children?

- Why is the father's plea for his children's heart the key to Christian parenting (Prov. 23:26)? How has your experience as a child influenced your thinking about this? Are there barriers in your heart that keep you from offering your heart to your children?

- If we compare a father's role with his children to a gardener's work among plants, how does this help you to think about your calling as a father?

- Do you think that the four words, Read, Pray, Work, and Play, are helpful in structuring time with your children? Which of these is most challenging to you?

- Have you made a commitment to family worship involving Scripture reading and prayer? Why is this so important?

- How can you display your passion for Jesus to your children? How can you make the Lord attractive to them?

Chapter 10

TO KEEP: THE DISCIPLINE OF CHILDREN

What would you think of a father who was responsible for raising the following boys?

- One son sexually assaults his half-sister, and is murdered by his brother in retaliation.
- This murdering son goes on to lead a rebellion against his father and is violently killed as a result.
- A third son later wages a rebellion against his father and a fourth brother, the designated heir.

Not quite the model family, is it? Where's the love and respect for Dear Old Dad? Would you consider the father of these thugs to be a paragon of spiritual leadership? Or even a halfway decent guy?

If you know the Bible well, you recognize this as a rough summary of the history of King David's sons. Yes, the "man after God's own heart" (1 Sam. 13:14), the author of at least seventy-five psalms. *That* King David.

In fact, if we look at the Bible's great men, what we are told about their sons is almost uniformly depressing. Jacob's sons hated their brother Joseph so much they wanted to murder him—until they realized they could get rid of him *and* gain a profit simply by selling him into slavery (see Gen. 37:18–28). Hophni and Phinehas, sons of the high priest Eli, were involved in repeated sexual sin so flagrant and shameless that it was publicly known among the Israelites, and they misused the animal sacrifices from the tabernacle at Shiloh for personal gain (see 1 Sam. 2:22–23, 27–29). So wicked were they that God destroyed their entire house. The prophet Samuel's sons were so corrupt that the elders of Israel sinned by demanding a "king like the nations" rather than be subjected to their leadership (1 Sam. 8:1–5). Even the great King Jehoshaphat, one of my personal heroes, made the classic mistake of allowing his son Jehoram to marry a daughter of the evil Ahab and Jezebel, with the predictable result that Jehoram "walked in the way of . . . the house of Ahab" (2 Kings 8:18).

Even worse is the case of King Hezekiah's son. Remember Hezekiah? He was the great king who prayed to the Lord during Sennacherib's siege so that the Assyrian army was completely wiped out beneath Jerusalem's walls (2 Kings 19). His son? None other than the Adolf Hitler of the Old Testament, King Manasseh, the perversely twisted leader who put statues of Molech in the Kidron Valley to make child sacrifice more user-friendly for the nation. Then there is the great reformer king, Josiah, the last righteous king of Judah. He was the *last* righteous king because all three of his sons ruled *un*righteously: Jehoiachin, Jehoiakim, and Zedekiah.

What is going on with these sons of heroes? Part of the answer, no doubt, is that great and powerful men typically don't have nearly enough time to win the hearts of their children, so the sons of kings often grow up into spoiled and rotten princes. Another issue was the Old Testament practice of polygamy, which resulted in kings' sons getting caught up in the petty rivalries and schemes of their inevitably insecure mothers. But how did David's family get to be the worst of all? How could so great a Bible hero as King David have such a colossal mess among his sons? The Bible answers clearly, saying of Adonijah (the third son in the scenario set out above), "his father had never at any time displeased him by asking, 'Why have you done thus and so?'" (1 Kings 1:6).

There it is. David failed to discipline his sons personally, never investing himself in the oversight of their proper conduct. The verse says "never," not "at any time." By this we see that David practically ensured that his sons would come to ruin. Of course, ruin, however suddenly it may manifest itself, emerges from a series of harmful events that accumulate over time. How is a father to minimize such harm in the lives of his children? The answer is a father's call to *keep* his children through the loving discipline that preserves them from harm.

THE CALL TO KEEP A CHILD'S HEART

According to the Bible, the gravest threat our children face is not physical—some mishap or assault (although these obviously can be real dangers). The gravest threat is spiritual—the dire threat of sin's power at work in their own hearts. The toxic youth culture we noted in the previous chapter, for example, is a threat only because our children have a sin nature that makes them susceptible to sin's influence. As David lamented, "Behold, I was brought forth in iniquity, and in sin did my mother conceive me" (Ps. 51:7). Appearances to the contrary, our children are born not "little angels," but little sinners. Ted Tripp elaborates: "There are things within the heart of the sweetest little baby that, allowed to blossom and grow to fruition, will bring about eventual destruction."[11]

Once again, it all comes down to the heart. Because of our sin nature, our heart poses threats to us all by itself. In addition, influences from outside us can harm by appealing to the power of sin inside us. But if we address a young person's *internal* sin problem—his heart—we also weaken the power of *external* sin problems. If our mandate to work in the garden of a child's life is meant to gain access to his heart and thus direct him to Christ, then it should come as no surprise that our mandate to keep is to protect that heart from seeking to satisfy its own sinful cravings.

Seek Obedience

Parental authority in the mode of keeping, therefore, has the obedience of our children as its immediate and urgent goal. In contrast with the values spread widely today, the Bible teaches that children are to obey their parents (Eph. 6:1) and parents are to rule their children. God said of Abraham, "I have chosen him, that he may command his children and his household after him to keep the way of the Lord by doing righteousness and justice" (Gen. 18:19). Abraham was to command his household in godly obedience to the Lord. This means that fathers, especially, are to make and enforce decisions with respect to their children.

This "keeping" of our children is not opposed to humility and love, for if we do not rule our children, sin certainly will. "The heart is deceitful above all things," Jeremiah said, "and desperately sick" (Jer. 17:9). Therefore, we do not permit our children to be ruled by their hearts but by their parents, representing (however imperfectly) God and His Word. "Discipline your son, and he will give you peace," says the proverb; "he will bring delight to your soul" (Prov. 29:17).

Exercise Self-Control

The granting of authority to fathers does not imply we have permission to mistreat our children. The Bible is clear in stating, "Fathers, do not provoke your children to anger, but bring them up in the discipline and instruction of the Lord" (Eph. 6:4). Children can be provoked to anger by a father in a variety of ways, all of which involve a failure of parental self-control. The most common way for a father to provoke his child to anger is by erupting in anger himself.

Anger is a serious issue for many fathers because a child's disobedience is seen as an affront to the father's authority and honor. But sinful displays of anger only undermine a father's authority, tempting a child to hold the father in disdain and contempt.

Notice how Ephesians 6:4 contrasts explosions of anger with the discipline of the Lord. Sinful anger and godly discipline, Paul is saying, are simply incompatible. To be effective fathers, therefore, we must master our emotions and control our speech, observing the warnings found in James 3. Sinful anger and harsh speech will only drive a wedge of fear and resentment between a father and his children. Parents are responsible to God for exercising parental authority, and fathers are responsible that the authority we exert is God-honoring and truly protective to our children.

THE WAY TO KEEP A CHILD'S HEART

There are two main ways in which parents act on their children to correct and restrain their sin. The first is physical punishment and the second is verbal reproof. To be a father is to be an authority figure who rules his children by commands and enforces his rules through the God-given means of corporal punishment and verbal correction. Our goal in all this is the same as that of God the Father in His fatherly discipline toward us: to produce "a harvest of righteousness and peace for those who have been trained by it" (Heb. 12:11).

Physical Reproof: Sparing Not the Rod

By physical punishment, I am referring to spanking. According to the Bible, spanking our young children is absolutely necessary to help restrain their sin and teach wisdom to their little hearts. The Bible says: "Do not withhold discipline from a child; if you strike him with a rod, he will not die. If you strike him with the rod, you will save his soul from Sheol" (Prov. 23:13–14). It adds, "The rod of correction imparts wisdom, but a child left to himself disgraces his mother" (Prov. 29:15). In fact, "Whoever spares the rod hates his son, but he who loves him is diligent to discipline him" (Prov. 13:14). Tripp writes that spanking "humbles the heart of a child, making him subject to parental instruction. . . . The spanking renders the child compliant and ready to receive life-giving words."[12]

It is extremely important that parents discipline their children in a controlled and highly intentional manner that will encourage repentance from the sin or other wrong behavior. The following points should prove helpful:

Seek privacy. Spanking should not be an exercise in public shaming, so it should be done privately.

Make the offense known. The child must be told specifically what he or she did that was wrong. Personally, I do not spank a child unless I have clearly communicated the broken rule in advance.

Require that the offense be acknowledged. The child must acknowledge the sinful behavior. After this, it is best if the child is told specifically the punishment he is about to receive and given a final reminder of why the punishment is necessary.

Embrace, reassure, and exhort. Then, after several hard spanks applied to the skin of the bottom—hard enough to sting but not hard enough to hurt[13]—the child should be embraced and reconciled, told of forgiveness of sin through the blood of Jesus Christ, and exhorted not to commit the sin again.

Repeat as necessary. The goal is a compliant child who acknowledges sin and accepts correction. Those who do not respond in this way should be spanked again, until their hearts yield.

Our goal is that through the way we administer spankings, and the attitude and demeanor we display, our children will conclude, "I shouldn't do that again," without ever thinking, "My father is mean and angry."

Spanking, properly conducted, will enable parents lovingly, immediately, and firmly to correct disobedience while opening the child's heart to instruction. A refusal or failure to "displease our children" (as 1 Kings 1:6 puts it) leads to unruly hearts and unhappy children.

I realize that our society increasingly teaches that spanking is immoral and harmful. Frankly, this view is nuts, and it is hateful to our children. I remember sitting on an airplane next to a man and his preschool-aged son. During the flight, the boy became increasingly obnoxious. He began thrashing and screaming, and when his father asked him to stop, the boy completely ignored him. After a while, the lad began slapping his father. Instead of disciplining him, the man tried to accommodate the boy and even buy him off with promises. Apparently pulling out the big guns, the father then threatened his son with "time out" when they got off the plane. None of it worked.

The whole thing was a pitiful and frustrating display of a failure of fatherly discipline. In the face of the boy's consistently petulant and miserable disobedience, I almost couldn't help offering, "Sir, would you mind if I took your son back to the restroom and spanked his bottom?" I even rehearsed my convincing appeal: "Really, I won't hurt him. I'm a trained father and the spanking will do him a world of good." I did not actually speak to the man, however. I doubted I'd receive a positive response. Even more importantly, I realized this rotten kid (with his politically correct father in tow) was merely my temporary frustration—not my son, not my responsibility, not my problem. But when it comes to my own children, whom I love and for whom I am accountable to God, I insist on biblical discipline for the restraint of their sin and the molding of their hearts.

Verbal Reproof: Exercising Parental Authority

All of this assumes that the father is to be, well, a father figure. Don't get me wrong: I have a great time with my five children (three girls and two boys, currently twelve and under) and we have a lot of fun together. But I'm not here just to be their pal. In fact, the only reason we can have so much fun together is because of the parental authority so vigorously exercised in their lives.

Being a father figure means imposing your will on your children by the force of your personality and authority. Of course, this is largely accomplished by your words. Fatherly authority does not derive from the fact that Dad is bigger (he may not always be, after all) but from God's command: "Children, obey your parents in the Lord, for this is right" (Eph. 6:1). Every Christian child should be drilled in this verse, so that the father's and mother's authority is grounded not in physical superiority but in divine command.

Consider the failure of Eli, Israel's high priest at the end of the period of the Judges. Eli had two sons who were the disgrace of Israel, Hophni and Phinehas. Eli allowed these corrupt ingrates to serve as priests at the tabernacle at Shiloh, where—as I mentioned a few pages back—they exploited their position for as much personal advantage as they could get. First Samuel 2:22 gives some of the grim facts: "Eli . . . kept hearing all that his sons were doing to all Israel, and how they lay with the women who were serving at the entrance to the tent of meeting." It is not that Eli never complained about his sons' wickedness: "He said to them, 'Why do you do such things? For I hear of your evil dealings with all the people'" (1 Sam. 2:23). But they just ignored him (a situation no father can afford to permit): "they would not listen to the voice of their father" (1 Sam. 2:25). Here was the root of Eli's failure: when his sons ignored him and went on sinning, he backed off, unwilling to enforce his fatherly authority.

What lay behind this gross parental failure? It occurs to me that we never read anything about a Mrs. Eli, so maybe the boys' mother died early in their lives (perhaps in childbirth?) and Eli was so sentimental about it that he wouldn't discipline the boys. Admittedly, this is speculation, though it is plausible. Or perhaps Eli felt guilty for neglecting them, being fairly busy as the high priest of Israel. Whatever the reason, it was no excuse for Eli's shortcomings. His failure to enforce his authority brought disaster on Israel, especially for his family (which God virtually wiped out because of these sins).

God was predictably angry that Eli allowed his sons to continue as priests serving in the tabernacle: "Why then do you scorn my sacrifices and my offerings that I commanded, and honor your sons above me . . . ?" (1 Sam. 2:29). At the battle of Ebenezer, the Lord was so disgusted when the wicked sons arrived with the ark of the covenant that God allowed the Philistines to wipe out the army and capture the ark. Wouldn't it have been better, we ask Eli, to stand up to your sons?

A father's authority is naturally demonstrated and exercised in a variety of ways. Sometimes just a look will communicate to our children what they need to understand at that moment. But, as I suggested above, the single most important manifestation of our authority, and the one to which we must pay the closest attention, is our speech. What we say to our children, and how we say it—most specifically how we reprove them verbally—is critical to the proper exercise of our God-given authority.

When it comes to exercising authority in this way, I confess I have been helped by the experience of being a tank officer in the Army. When I was 21, I was a tank platoon leader with sergeants who were all many years older, so I had to learn to speak in a command voice. This is not to be confused with yelling or whining—it is commanding. When giving commands to our children, fathers should speak in a firm, authoritative voice (it doesn't even have to be loud, just decisive) so that the sinful hearts of our children are not confused about the option of disobeying. Children should be trained to respond to their father's commands, with the expectation of prompt obedience. This requires fathers to enforce compliance, which is where spanking comes in. Children who have been trained to obey the sound of their father's voice are those whose hearts are compliant toward all proper authority. Such submission to authority is a prerequisite to success in life, which is why father figures are so important to children and society.

Even as I write this, I imagine some readers, trained by popular psychobabble, rolling their eyes at this emphasis on command voice and enforced obedience. These are signs, many believe today, of an insecure male ego. But according to God's Word, they are the signs of a father who loves his children. Children who are commanded by their fathers are happy and confident, especially when the father has proven his love and his commands are guided by the precepts of God's Word. Such children are not left to their own devices, which are inevitably inept and unwise (see Prov. 22:15), but are having their wills trained to obey the good and perfect counsel of the Holy Scriptures.

ADVICE ON APPLICATION

When it comes to raising children, what is keeping all about? That is, what do we seek to protect our children from? First, we protect them from the internal threat—their own folly and sin—and second, we protect them from the external threat—the ways of an increasingly dangerous culture.

We protect them from *internal* threats through physical punishment (the rod) and by the exercise of verbal reproof. This is never fun. I would much rather be lazy, clueless, and indulgent toward my children. In some ways, it would be much easier to be like that father on the plane—driven in fear from my God-given place of fatherly authority by the foolishness of humanistic blather. But, you see, I love my children, and I have been taught what it means to exercise fatherly love according to the biblical pattern. Therefore, I count it among my highest honors before God to seek to exercise that authority as I should.

When it comes to *external* threats, we protect our children in a variety of ways and situations. Of course, fathers are to protect their children against any and all physical threats. Fathers are also to protect their children from morally harmful influences. This includes denying them access to certain video games and various types of Internet sites, as well as a large percentage of secular movies and television programs.

Fathers are also to protect their children from unwholesome relationships. When our children came of school age, my wife and I considered the possibility of our local public schools. During our visit, we learned that some of the teachers were Christians and that the prevailing secular culture was somewhat countered by believing influences. But as I lay awake at night thinking and praying about it, all I could think of was the opening verse of Psalm 1: "Blessed is the man who walks not in the counsel of the wicked, nor stands in the way of sinners, nor sits in the seat of scoffers" (Ps. 1:1). I am their father, and I cannot allow my children to walk in the counsel of the wicked, so far as I am able. This clarified our thinking when it came to schooling options. Other parents may come to a different conclusion than we did, but they cannot delegate the responsibility to guard their children's hearts.

This twofold duty of defending our children against threats both internal and external is a basic obligation of fathers toward their children, an obligation that centers on bringing discipline into their lives. Let me conclude, then, with some practical advice for fathers on disciplining children.

Be the Bad Cop

First, as much as possible, the father should try to be the bad cop, that is, the more stern disciplinarian compared with the mother. In most cases, our wives spend much of their lives with our children. Especially when children are young, this can involve exercising correction almost constantly. It is pretty tough for our wives to swallow, then, if we fathers show up at the end of the workday and play the role of the happy-go-lucky non-disciplinarian.

When I arrive on the scene, I do not want my wife to think, "O great, there goes the discipline!" Instead, I want her to say: "What a relief! I can relax a bit now that Rick is around." Moreover, it is a real help to her in her seasons of constant discipline if she can wield the threat of my involvement (and my harder spanking). Moms get worn down, and familiarity can breed contempt on the part of the kids. So it really helps our wives if they can say, "Keep this up and your father will learn of it!" If the children turn pale at the thought of this—because you are a godly father rather than an angry one—something very good is happening.

Maintain a Sense of Humor

A sense of humor is a huge help in wielding authority and exercising discipline. To the extent there is a heaviness in the air, our authority seems harsh and impersonal. But if the overall environment is lighthearted and happy, children recognize the contrast when it comes to punishment, and their sense of their parents' overall goodwill is thereby enhanced. As we saw in the previous chapter, parenting requires a bonded relationship with children, and in this as in all things, "a joyful heart is good medicine" (Prov. 17:22). Fathers who are tender and kind to their children will find them generally more receptive to the exercise of authority. Likewise, I advise overall courtesy in parents' speech to their children. It does not at all undermine my authority to say "Please" and "Thank you" to my kids—in fact, it enhances it. By showing them respect, we encourage our children to give respect, both to us and to others.

Do Not Provoke

This is worth reemphasizing because it is such a consistent area of temptation for many fathers (and mothers). Let us always remember that Paul's command, "Fathers, do not provoke your children to anger" (Eph. 6:4), is tied to the command for our children to obey us. We cannot in integrity emphasize the command given to children without equally emphasizing the command given to us.

In order to avoid provoking our children to anger, we must be fair and judicious in placing demands on our boys and girls. We should not be personally abusive (again, all abuse undermines rather than enhances authority). I want my children to think of themselves with God-given dignity and self-respect, and this requires the proper praise and respect of their father toward them.

Here's a rule I try very hard to follow: *I will always be on my children's side, even if I am punishing. I will never be against them and I will never speak to them with contempt.* To my regret, I have broken this rule more than once. So what do fathers do when they sin against their children? They should confess their sin to their children and ask their forgiveness, treating them as Christians worthy of truth and grace.

Part of being fair and judicious toward our children includes having reasonable expectations. Our children should not be punished for well-intentioned failures or for developmental limitations. Punishment must be reserved for willful disobedience.

For instance, when my youngest son was in second grade, my wife and I believed that his Christian school teacher had unrealistic expectations about the ability of some little boys to sit still in the classroom. Our son is by nature a bit of a daydreamer, which his parents do not consider a liability (although sometimes it is a challenge). After our son's first week of school, during which he was berated for exhibiting the traits of the seven-year-old boy he was, the teacher called me to insist that I punish my son. I asked her to outline his disobedience. When she did and we discussed it, even she had to admit that none of his disobedience constituted willful rebellion. I politely refused to punish my son, believing the problem lay with the teacher's

TO KEEP: THE DISCIPLINE OF CHILDREN

failure to observe Ephesians 6:4 (in her delegated role as a temporary, quasi-parental authority).

I remember very well sitting down with my cowed and terrified son that weekend. He had been beaten down all week and now assumed his father was going to let him have it. Instead, I informed him that I did not think he deserved punishment and that I expected him to do his best while respecting his teacher at all times. Then I prayed with him that God would help him to obey his teacher as well as he could. I am certain this meant a lot to my son, who saw that his father was trying to be honest and fair, and that his parents were on his side.

It was a long year for my son, as his teacher never warmed to him for a variety of reasons. But as we prayed with him throughout the year and urged his best efforts at obeying, it strengthened our relationship. This was a lesson for me that part of exercising fatherly authority is ensuring that standards and expectations for our children are right and that their treatment is as fair as possible.

Bathe It All in Prayer

Finally, if it is not obvious that all our parenting efforts must be bathed in prayer, then we do not understand the difficulty of the challenge! Consider the example of King David. He was a true spiritual giant, yet when he neglected his sons the result was sheer disaster. What will be the results from my own sins and failures as a father? I tremble to consider them, but I turn to 1 Peter 5:6–7 as my consolation: "Humble yourselves, therefore, under the mighty hand of God so that at the proper time he may exalt you, casting all your anxieties on him, because he cares for you."

God cares for us fathers (as he does mothers), the Bible says, and that makes all the difference. So parents should practically live by prayer, casting our many anxieties for our children into His loving hands, remembering the Lord's covenant faithfulness and His own commitment to our children. For just as God promised to Abraham, He promises to us: "I will establish my covenant between me and you and your offspring after you throughout their generations for an everlasting covenant, to be God to you and to your offspring after you" (Gen. 17:7). It is in this hope that we love our children by exercising fatherly discipline—the very love by which our heavenly Father "disciplines us for good, that we may share in his holiness" (Heb. 12:10).

Questions for Reflection and Discussion

- Reflect on the list of Old Testament saints who failed to raise godly children. What do you make of this? What factors might have contributed to this tendency?

- How do you feel about the idea of parental authority? Do you agree that a father must be an authority figure who enforces his rule?

- What do you think about the biblical methods for punishing children? Do you have tips for what to do and what not to do? Why is such discipline increasingly opposed in secular society?

- Why is it important for fathers to treat their children with courtesy, kindness and good humor even while exercising authority? Why do men sometimes struggle with anger when disciplining their children? Why is it important to restrain anger, and how do men do this?

Chapter 11

MEN
IN FRIENDSHIP

There are two statues in Washington, D.C., that together tell a remarkable story. One is the massive memorial to General Ulysses S. Grant that stands at the east end of the Reflecting Pool, literally in the morning shadow of the U.S. Capitol building. Visitors can hardly miss this majestic depiction of the legendary general atop his war stallion. Grant's military leadership was decisive to the Union's victory in the Civil War, and he is considered a symbol of the force of human will, an icon of the strong man who stands against the storm when all others have shrunk back. This prominently displayed monument was erected by his grateful, admiring generation as a celebration of his unique contributions.

Some two and a half miles away, in a pleasant but small and nondescript city park, stands a more commonplace memorial. The statue of this lesser-known Civil War figure Major General John Rawlins has actually had eight different locations and is hardly ever noticed by visitors. Rawlins had been a lawyer in

Galena, Illinois, where Grant lived just prior to the war, and he became Grant's chief of staff. Rawlins knew Grant's character flaws, especially his weakness for alcohol. At the beginning of the war, Rawlins extracted a pledge from Grant to abstain from drunkenness, and when the general threatened to fall away from that promise, his friend would plead with him and support him until Grant could get back on track. In many ways, it was Rawlins who stood beside the seemingly solitary figure of Grant the great general. Rawlins' memorial is modest compared with the mounted glory afforded Grant, yet without his unheralded love and support, Grant would hardly have managed even to climb into the saddle.

It is the Grant statue that adorns postcards sold in the Capitol bookstore; no one pays the least attention to Rawlins. Ours is a world that celebrates the individual—the power of one, solitary achievements, and individual laurels. But the Bible sees things from a very different perspective. The wise man of Ecclesiastes says: "Two are better than one, because they have a good reward for their toil. For if they fall, one will lift up his fellow. But woe to him who is alone when he falls and has not another to lift him up!" (Eccl. 4:9–10).

THE REMARKABLE JONATHAN

In our study of manhood and the Bible's Masculine Mandate to work and keep, it is obvious why we focused first on marriage and fatherhood. These are the personal relationships that dominate a man's life. But they are not the only relationships a man is to enjoy. One mark of a true godly man is his faithfulness in friendship to other men, especially to Christian brothers. The Bible celebrates the true friend, and most of us find that godly male companions are among the most blessed resources in life.

If the friendship between Grant and Rawlins is a great American story, perhaps the greatest friendship recorded in Scripture is the brotherly love between Jonathan and David. The two men met early in life, in the aftermath of David's famous victory over the Philistine giant Goliath. First Samuel 17 tells how the entire Israelite host cowered in terror before this fearsome champion, and how the shepherd boy, shielded only by his faith in God and armed with only a slingshot, struck down the Philistine and led Israel to victory. Jonathan was the son and heir of Israel's King Saul, and the hero of earlier battles. In fact, Jonathan had been the darling of Israel's army prior to David's explosive appearance on the scene. How natural (in sin) it would have been for Jonathan to resent the upstart youth. Yet exactly the opposite happened, for Jonathan presents one of the most beautiful portrayals of manly grace in all of Scripture. First Samuel 18:1 simply records, "the soul of Jonathan was knit to the soul of David, and Jonathan loved him as his own soul." In David, not only had the Lord found "a man after his own heart" (1 Sam. 13:14), but godly Jonathan had found one, too.

It is not by chance that I have a son named Jonathan, for the Old Testament Jonathan is one of the few men in Scripture of whom there are no recorded vices. We read nothing in all the accounts of Jonathan to suggest anything but a heart filled with faith in the Lord and love for God's people. This does not mean Jonathan had no sin; as a relatively minor figure in the

Bible, he does not get very extensive treatment. But it is worth noting that this man who is considered the greatest of friends was also a man of vibrant faith and purity of heart.

From a worldly perspective, we would expect Jonathan to be the most bitter of David's enemies. As prince, Jonathan stood to inherit the throne of his father, so David's rise threatened his dynasty. Yet when David defeated Goliath, Jonathan seems to have understood that God was providing David in the place of Saul and his family. Jonathan responded by taking off his own royal robe, along with his sword, bow, and belt, and placing them on the rising champion, thus presenting young David before the veteran troops. Why did he act this way? Jonathan "loved him as his own soul" (1 Sam. 18:3), because Jonathan loved the Lord and loved the faith he saw burning in young David.

Later, when David's growing popularity earned him the paranoid hatred of King Saul, it was Jonathan who intervened to save David's life, even though he knew it would cast him under his father's suspicion. Ultimately, David was forced to flee and gather a war band of his own. For years, Saul pursued David, wearing away at his faith and resolve. Although David was sustained throughout this time by God's promise that he would be made king, he grew weary amid the toll of exile and persecution. It was during this time in David's life, when he seems to have been on the brink of despair and defeat, that Jonathan came and provided a model of manly friendship.

THE FRIEND WHO COMES

David had found refuge from Saul in the caves of Adullam, in central Judea. He left his fortress, however, to rescue the citizens of a nearby town who had been beset by the Philistines. Saul learned of David's movements and pounced to capture David and his men before they could return to the safety of Adullam. Saul's rapid advance drove David and his forces far into the southern desert, hotly pursued by the king's superior forces.

We read of David's dire situation in 1 Samuel 23: "David remained in the strongholds in the wilderness, in the hill country of the wilderness of Ziph. And Saul sought him every day, but God did not give him into his hand" (v. 14). By this time David had been running from Saul for several years. We can imagine his extreme weariness and how slim his hold on God's promises of salvation must have been at times. No wonder this is the man who wrote: "My soul is in anguish. How long, O Lord, how long!" (Ps. 6:3 NIV).

It was at just this time that Jonathan returned to David. It seems that he had been serving as a commander in Saul's army. Becoming aware of David's increasingly desperate position, Jonathan acted to provide one of the classic examples of faithful friendship. The Bible expresses this in these brief but potent words: "Jonathan, Saul's son, rose and went to David at Horesh, and strengthened his hand in God" (1 Sam. 23:16). How loaded with implications is this simple statement.

Taking Initiative

For starters, Jonathan took the initiative and went to David. This was an act of sacrificial ministry. Safe at the side of his father and within the strong ranks of the pursuing army, Jonathan departed to expose himself to the danger David was experiencing. From the comfort of the king's royal provision, he ventured out into the desert deprivation of his friend. This is what friendship requires. A friend who is not willing, and even eager, to sacrifice time, labor, and hardship is not worthy of being called a friend at all.

Seeking to Understand

Second, Jonathan was sensitive to the needs of his friend. Many of us would be willing to make sacrifices if we only understood the real needs of others. But this would require us to do what Jonathan did: to think through what David must be experiencing. Jonathan was not focused on his own hardship, the difficult situation his friendship with David created for him, or the danger to his career aspirations. Instead, Jonathan committed his own needs to the Lord and gave his thoughts to the plight of his friend, David. This is the kind of thing Paul had in mind when he wrote to the Philippians: "Do nothing from rivalry or conceit, but in humility count others more significant than yourselves. Let each of you look not only to his own interests, but also to the interests of others" (Phil. 2:3–4).

Consider David's predicament. He was the leader of a band of weary fugitives, stranded in the desert. David was paying the price of leadership, his own thoughts given over to his men and their needs, while he stood alone with no peers or companions for himself. While David lent his strength to others, there were none to uphold him in his weakness. Consider, today, a doctor or nurse providing care to the desperately sick: who is there to uphold and encourage the caregiver? Or consider a mother spending herself for her little children, or a weary pastor fretting over his flock. What friend will come alongside, seeking to understand and to minister out of that understanding? Jonathan knew how great is the gift of companionship to a struggling friend.

The Bible says that God was not willing to give David up to Saul. But do you think David was consistently confident of this? Wouldn't David have found this hard to see in such a time of trial? There he was in a hostile land with a royal enemy hot on his heels. David could really use some signs of God's faithfulness, encouraging him to believe and continue the fight. And God was about to provide that encouragement in the form of a true friend.

Jonathan went to David in his place of struggle. In the same way, our friendship today means little if we will not seek out and find our brothers in their places of need. "A friend loves at all times," says the proverb, "and a brother is born for adversity" (Prov. 17:17).

THE HELPING HAND

It would have meant a great deal to David just to see his faithful friend Jonathan in such a time and place of need. But Jonathan did more than show up: he did for David the single thing most needed in troubling times. The Bible puts it simply: "Jonathan . . . strengthened his hand in God" (1 Sam. 23:16). David's hand was trembling and in danger of slipping from the strong support that is our faith in God. Jonathan came and strengthened the grip of David's faith and hope in the Lord.

Do you ever wonder how to encourage a struggling friend? It is a great thing to come and take another by the hand. But it is something even greater to take that shaking hand and rest it secure on the promises of God. This is exactly what Jonathan did for David: "He said to him, 'Do not fear, for the hand of Saul my father shall not find you. You shall be king over Israel, and I shall be next to you. Saul my father also knows this'" (1 Sam. 23:17).

At the very moment Jonathan said this, his father's army was bearing down on David. So on what basis did he speak this way? Jonathan spoke from his memory of the promises God had made to David, promises that were certain to be fulfilled. We might paraphrase Jonathan's encouragement in this way: "Look, David, don't fail to put your trust in God. Remember the Lord's promise that you will be king. But in case you are doubting, let me share something with you. Even my father Saul knows that this is how it will all end up. So don't fear Saul, David, but trust the Lord!"

What a timely message this was! The Jonathans of this world are few and far apart. They are the hero's heroes, and surely precious to God's own heart.

This is what the prophet Elisha did for his companion when surrounded by enemy horsemen: "Do not be afraid, for those who are with us are more than those who are with them." When the man expressed his doubt, Elisha prayed the best of prayers, one that answers our most pressing need: "O LORD, please open his eyes that he may see" (2 Kings 6:16–17).

Dietrich Bonhoeffer knew the value of godly friendship in the midst of danger. A rising evangelical scholar who had outspokenly opposed Hitler, Bonhoeffer had been persuaded to work outside Germany, so that during the early years of Nazi domination he lived safely in England. But Bonhoeffer knew that his friends and congregation needed his presence and his personal appeals to faith. Returning to Nazi Germany, he led an underground seminary, where he lived together with faithful Christian men preparing to minister in that difficult situation, until his opposition to Hitler ultimately led to his arrest and execution. In *Life Together*, a book recounting his experience in that secret Christian community, Bonhoeffer wrote:

> The Christian needs another Christian who speaks God's Word to him. He needs him again and again when he becomes uncertain and discouraged. . . . He needs his brother man as a bearer and proclaimer of the divine word of salvation. . . . And that also clarifies the goal of all Christian community: they meet one another as bringers of the message of salvation.[14]

MINISTERING TO FAITH

Jonathan's example with David shows us that a godly friend ministers primarily to the faith of his brothers in Christ, seeking to build up their trembling hearts and protect them from the dangers of unbelief and fear. This is the Genesis 2:15 work-and-keep mandate at work in the important arena of male friendship. When we come to a friend and "strengthen his hand in God," we restore his wavering faith to its certain confidence in the unfailing promises of the Lord.

Jonathan's intervention proved to be a real turning point for David, that great man of God. What a difficult time this was for David. He had just experienced a bitter betrayal, and it was about to happen again. First, after he had exposed his forces by rescuing the town of Keilah from the Philistines, the people responded by reporting his presence to King Saul (1 Sam. 23:12–14). Now, in the desert where David was trying to hide, the Ziphites were actively negotiating his betrayal to Saul (1 Sam. 23:19). Yet there was one shining light in this darkness, the spiritual help given by Jonathan, who strengthened David's hand in God. Through that one friend's loving aid, David found courage to go on by hoping in the Lord. It is in this way that the words of Proverbs 18:19 (NIV) are found true: "A brother helped is like a strong city." Jonathan's loyal friendship was a crucial support that propped up the sagging walls of David's spirit.

It was shortly after Jonathan's intervention that David was able to lift his heart with the words of Psalm 57:1: "Be merciful to me, O God, be merciful to me, for in you my soul takes refuge; in the shadow of your wings I will take refuge, till the storms of destruction pass by." Jonathan had reminded and encouraged David to look for God's help not in the caves of Adullam or the desert hideout of Ziph, but in the Rock that is our God. In that fortress of security, David could sing with joy: "My heart is steadfast, O God, my heart is steadfast!" (Ps. 57:7).

Of course, God did deliver David. The Ziphites betrayed David to King Saul, but then, just as Saul had nearly trapped the fugitives and it seemed that David's cause was lost, news reached the king of a sudden Philistine attack into Israel: "As Saul and his men were closing in on David and his men to capture them, a messenger came to Saul, saying, 'Hurry and come, for the Philistines have made a raid against the land.' So Saul returned from pursuing after David and went against the Philistines" (1 Sam. 23:26–28).

Without the faithful friendship of Jonathan, who loved God and therefore loved his believing friend even as he loved himself, David easily could have given up hope. But Jonathan went to David, having given sympathetic thought to David's likely needs. When he arrived, he spoke words that built up David's faith, "strengthening his hand in God," so that David no longer tottered in unbelief but gained a steady hold on God's unfailing truth. The best friend is always one who turns our hearts to rest upon the Lord. How greatly we ought to treasure true friends in Christ. And how greatly we ought to desire to be such a friend. One of the best ways for us to serve the Lord, to reflect His glory in the world and fulfill God's calling on us as men, is to step off the sidelines of life, to offer our time and compassion to friends in need, and to speak words of truth and grace that lead them to (or back to) the Lord. In this way, we will also grow more and more in the likeness of Jesus Christ ourselves.

Scripture says, "there is a friend who sticks closer than a brother" (Prov. 18:24), and the ultimate example of that friend is the Son of God who willingly died to free us from our sins. Like Jonathan, Jesus came from a place of safety into our world of hardship and danger. Like Jonathan, Jesus left riches and comfort to enter into our poverty. He not only strengthened our hand in God, he brought us into a saving relationship with God through His blood. Jesus says to us, "I will never leave you nor forsake you" (Heb. 13:5). We, therefore, serve Jesus well when we stand by our friends, speak to them the words that strengthen faith, and, in Christ's name, share in their troubles and sorrows. If we will be true friends to our brothers in Christ, then what was said to Christ's glory may also be said of us: "Greater love has no one than this, that someone lay down his life for his friends" (John 15:13).

Questions for Reflection and Discussion

- Do friendships with other men play an important role in your life? If so, how? If not, why do you think this is?

- Consider Jonathan's sacrificial ministry in *going to* David. Why was this so important? What are some barriers that keep Christian men from being present in the lives of friends? Can you think of some steps that will enable you to have a greater presence in the lives of male friends and to allow them to be more present in your life?

- Have you ever given help to a Christian friend who was struggling with his faith? Have you ever received such help? What was effective in ministering to such a person? What does the Bible mean in saying that Jonathan "strengthened David's hand in God"? Why is this such an essential ministry to friends in need?

- Jonathan was able to minister so effectively to David because he had been thinking about his friend's situation and had become sensitive to his needs. What are some ways you can make yourself more sensitive to the needs of your male friends so as to intercede for them in the presence of God?

Chapter 12

THE MASCULINE MANDATE IN THE CHURCH

When Nehemiah went to Jerusalem to supervise the rebuilding of its walls, the city was in a condition many considered hopeless. To make matters worse, there were enemies lurking outside, waiting for any opportunity to strike and tear down what Israel was trying to build. In light of these twin challenges, Nehemiah directed the men to two kinds of tasks, as indicated in the book that bears his name: "half of my servants worked on construction, and half held spears, shields, bows, and coats of mail" (Neh. 4:16).

What do we see here? Once again, God's Genesis 2:15 pattern is crystal clear: Nehemiah's men *worked*, laboring to build the walls, and they *kept*, standing guard to protect both the workers and the work already accomplished. In demonstrating the use of the Masculine Mandate among God's people collectively, Nehemiah set a precedent that holds even today. Within the church, men are called to work and keep in service to God. That is, Christian men are to labor in the church with the trowel in one hand (Adam's gardening trowel and Nehemiah's brick mason's trowel supplemented by the "trowels" of a thousand other professions and pursuits) and with the sword of truth (which never really changes) in the other hand. Under such servant-laborers and the guardian care of godly men, Christ's church grows strong and remains safe for its mission of spreading the gospel in the world.

MALE-ONLY LEADERSHIP

It is necessary to state up front that authoritative positions of leadership in the New Testament church are to be held only by men. Women can and should play leading roles in the church, for a church with a strong masculine presence will have a strong feminine beauty about it as well. But the positions of authority—the roles of teaching and ruling—are restricted to men. To become convinced of the truth and authority of Scripture, and then to read the plain words of the New Testament, is to come to this conclusion easily and naturally.

The offices of spiritual authority within the church are those of the elders and the deacons. The elders oversee all the affairs of the church, attending especially to its spiritual well-being, while the deacons exercise authority over the physical interests of the church and lead in the ministry of good works (see Acts 6:1–6). The qualifications for elders and deacons are set out by Paul in 1 Timothy 3:1–13, where gender-specific statements make it clear that these offices are intended by God only for males.[15]

Paul states the general principle of male headship in 1 Corinthians 11:3–9: "I want you to understand that the head of every man is Christ, the head of a wife is her husband, and the head of Christ is God. . . . For man was not made from woman, but woman from man. Neither was man created for woman, but woman for man" (1 Cor. 11:3, 8–9). This principle of male leadership is also specifically applied to the exercise of governing authority and teaching in the church. Paul writes to Timothy, "I do not permit a woman to teach or to exercise authority over a man; rather, she is to remain quiet" (1 Tim. 2:12). Again, Paul grounds this teaching on the design of God in creation and also on the effects of the fall (1 Tim. 2:13–14). Moreover, the fact that Jesus appointed only men to the apostolate, and that the early church elected only men to the first diaconate, sets a precedent that we have no reason to set aside.

In other New Testament passages, women are encouraged in their teaching of children and of other women. But the foundational message about teaching and the exercise of spiritual authority within the church as a whole is clear: these roles are reserved for Christian men. To the degree that men fail to assume these roles gladly and exercise them diligently, we end up with feminized churches that can quickly become fruitless and unsound because they are not being led as God intended.

Equipped for Service

What does this say to Christian men in the church? For one thing, it says that men should be serious about their faith so as to equip themselves to serve in church leadership. Not all men can or should serve as elders or deacons. But the church has and always will have a profound need for qualified, godly men to serve and lead. Therefore, a faithful Christian man should prepare himself to serve in such a capacity.

A man who senses a call to Christian ministry should examine 1 Timothy 3:2–7 closely, for it is here that Paul explicitly sets out the biblical qualifications for church office. Following are some key phrases from that passage accompanied by my attempts to elaborate, emphasize, and apply:

"An overseer must be above reproach" (v. 2). He should labor to ensure that his life casts a good light on Christ and His church.

He should be "able to teach" (v. 2). He must ensure that he is sound in the faith and able to convey it to others (this is as necessary for fatherhood as for eldership).

An overseer should be "sober-minded, self-controlled, respectable . . . not a drunkard, not violent but gentle" (vv. 2–3). He should be growing in Christlike godliness, showing the fruit of the Spirit and gaining control over his passions.

An overseer should be "not quarrelsome, not a lover of money" (v. 3). He should be advancing in sanctification so that the biblical values of peace and contentment are evident in his life.

"He must manage his own household well, with all dignity keeping his children submissive" (v. 4). He should be practicing the faith in his home and thus learning to lead in the church.

"He must be well thought of by outsiders, so that he may not fall into disgrace" (v. 7). He should live so as to have good relations with non-Christians and a reputation for integrity.

Our churches today need men who address life with this kind of purpose, striving to prepare themselves and grow spiritually so they are qualified to serve as leaders in the flock of the Lord Jesus.

All Are Soldiers, Athletes, Farmers

But there is something else we must notice about the biblical phrases I listed above. As we look at the 1 Timothy 3 biblical qualifications for church office, we see a handbook for the kind of godliness to which *all* Christian men should aspire. Set out for us there is an excellent agenda for any Christian man to follow: personal godliness, self-control, knowledge of truth, and a good reputation within and outside the church. What a blessing it is to lead such a life—and how uncommon it is today! Those of us who were converted in adulthood (as I was) remember when these things could not be said of us, and rejoice at the work of Christ in our lives for His glory.

Indeed, Paul calls each Christian man to be "a good soldier

of Christ Jesus" (2 Tim. 2:3), and the first battle we face as believers is with our own sinful habits and spiritual immaturity. Paul also compares us to athletes training for a victor's crown, and to hard-working farmers producing a good crop. The contest of our lives is that of godliness, and the field in which we first plow and plant is our own character and heart, through devotion to the Word of God, prayer, and a sincere application of God's grace to the affairs of our lives. Christian men who are not yet called into formal church office should never complain that they have nothing to do. We all have much to do in our own hearts and lives, and the requirement for well-qualified men to serve as leaders in the church is always urgent and vital.

WORKER-BUILDERS IN THE CHURCH

The calling of Christian men to work in the church includes the ideas of building and strengthening the body of believers. This is the first aspect of the Masculine Mandate, the calling to *work*. Ephesians 4:7–16 gives us the New Testament model for growing the church, beginning with the gifts that the risen and exalted Christ gives to His people from heaven: "grace was given to each one of us," Paul writes, "according to the measure of Christ's gift" (Eph. 4:7). This raises a question that Christian men should seek to answer: *What particular kinds of work is Christ calling me to do in the church, for which He has given me particular spiritual gifting?* The New Testament letters list such gifts as serving, teaching, exhorting, helping, generosity, leadership, mercy, and administration (Rom. 12:6–8; 1 Cor.

12:28).[16] These should not be taken as an exhaustive list or even a formal one, but rather as the kinds of things Christ equips us to do by the power of the Holy Spirit. Each of us should have a sense of our spiritual gifts and be busy putting them to work in the church, since the gifts were given by the Lord for the sake of His people.

Make Yourself Available

My advice to new believers, or to men who have not previously sought to serve in the church, is neither novel nor difficult to follow. It is simply this: keep alert for any need that comes up and that you have some ability and desire to take on, and offer to meet it.

Shortly after I was converted, my church announced a tutoring ministry to inner-city youth. I thought this would be a valuable ministry and one I could serve in passably well, so I asked about getting involved. As it turned out, serving in this ministry was challenging and required a combination of hard work and God's grace. Yet the Lord greatly blessed me through it. In fact, in important ways my subsequent life of service to the Lord has been built upon the gifts and abilities He revealed in me as I was willing to step up and meet this need.

Later, when I was teaching at a university, I was asked to participate in evangelistic Bible studies for students. Because this matched a desire I had to work for the salvation of others, I gladly got involved. Within a few years, the Lord called me to change my career and serve Him full-time as a preacher.

My experiences are hardly unique; God often calls and

directs us in such ways. Most often, spiritual gifts are revealed not through a diagnostic test but through the experience of serving the Lord. The sooner we begin serving where there is a need, the sooner we will begin to learn where the Lord is leading us in our service to Him.

The Centrality of Teaching

Further on in Ephesians 4, Paul says that God has a specific and important role for the ordained teachers and leaders of the church: "he gave the apostles, the prophets, the evangelists, the shepherds and teachers, to equip the saints for the work of ministry, for building up the body of Christ" (Eph. 4:11–12). What is the one thing all these ministers have in common? Their labor focuses on the communication of God's Word.

Today—because the apostles and prophets were provided only for the apostolic age prior to the writing of the New Testament—Christians are especially led by shepherd/teachers, generally called pastors or preachers. As these men minister God's Word to equip the believers, the believers themselves engage in the "work of ministry . . . building up the body of Christ." This ministry can involve many things, including personal evangelism, teaching in various settings, serving as a deacon or elder, handling administrative or practical matters, overseeing church finances, and more.

Building up the body of Christ also includes our ministry to one another. Consider these statements, all of which involve ways in which we teach and remind one another of what is true:

> If anyone is caught in any transgression, you who are spiritual should restore him in a spirit of gentleness. . . . Bear one another's burdens, and so fulfill the law of Christ. (Gal. 6:1–2)

> We urge you, brothers, admonish the idle, encourage the fainthearted, help the weak, be patient with them all. (1 Thess. 5:14)

> Exhort one another every day, as long as it is called "today," that none of you may be hardened by the deceitfulness of sin. (Heb. 3:13)

Just as we are all called to play our part in building the church corporately, we are all called to build up one another in the faith. Here is where the kind of manly friendship we discussed in Chapter 11 plays such an important role in the church. Christian men need friends who can strengthen their hand in God, and they need to be such a friend to others.

Through His Word, Christ provides all that His people need. Faithful preaching and teaching of the mighty, holy, and lifegiving Word of God equip the saints for the work of ministry and build up the church. To describe the result of it all, Paul concludes with challenging words that speak of what we are aiming for together in the ministry of the church: "until we all attain to the unity of the faith and of the knowledge of the Son of God, to mature manhood, to the measure of the stature of the fullness of Christ" (Eph. 4:13).

Know the Word

So it is the Word of God—by the grace of God taught, heard, understood, and applied—that accomplishes all progress within a church. From this, one conclusion is abundantly clear: any Christian man who wants to serve the Lord, in any role and at any level, must begin by devoting himself to God's Word. A man who is weak in the Word of God will be of little use for service, for we cannot truly serve God effectively in our own knowledge and strength. But God's Word stirs up in us the faith and spiritual strength needed to serve Him.

A growing understanding of Scripture is best gained by a lifestyle of daily Bible study and reflection. Psalm 1 says of the "blessed man" that "his delight is in the law of the LORD, and on his law he meditates day and night. He is like a tree planted by streams of water that yields its fruit in its season, and its leaf does not wither. In all that he does, he prospers" (vv. 1–3). This speaks of spiritual prospering, so that a man who is devoted to God's Word becomes strong for the work of the Lord. The fact that the entire book of Psalms begins with this statement tells us that this is the urgent priority for any man who would grow strong in the Lord and be useful to His church.

By equipping ourselves to be strong in the Word, by using the gifts that Christ has granted to us, and by ministering to one another in truth and love, we build the church of Christ together. Christian men are therefore to be like Nehemiah's workers, who built up Jerusalem in that ancient day. Peter says that this is the labor of the royal priesthood of all believers, called into service by Jesus through His blood that they might display His glory in the world and do the work of His gospel: "you yourselves like living stones are being built up as a spiritual house, to be a holy priesthood, to offer spiritual sacrifices acceptable to God through Jesus Christ" (1 Peter 2:5). Having been built together as a house by Christ, we in turn unite to build Christ's house, the church, as we serve in whatever ways we are equipped and called.

KEEPER-PROTECTORS IN THE CHURCH

My wife will tell you that her favorite worship services are those in which new elders or deacons are ordained and installed. She always beams when a crowd of men goes to the front to ordain new church leaders by the laying on of hands in the apostolic fashion. Almost without fail, she will say to me sometime during that day: "I love seeing all those spiritual and godly men who lead our church. It makes me feel like a woman, and it makes me feel safe in the church."

When my wife makes these comments, she is experiencing the fulfillment of the second part of the Masculine Mandate in the church, the calling to *keep*. We are not only to labor for the growth and health of the church, but we are to stand watch for the safekeeping of the church and its people. Like Nehemiah's builders, some working and some guarding, and like Adam in the garden, called to wield both the gardener's trowel and the warrior's sword, Christian men are called to safeguard the church even as we are laboring to build it up. And what are we to protect? When Paul wrote Timothy about the leadership of the church, he directed that the elders safeguard the church's *practice* and *doctrine* (see 1 Tim. 1:3–7).

Protect Church Practice

The practice of the church involves not merely its formal activities, such as worship services, but also the church's spirituality. Men in the church are to stand up to ensure that people are treated as they should be and to look out for those who are left out or cast down. When a destructive influence such as gossip and division besets the church, godly men should step in to put a stop to it. Moreover, sinful trends that dominate in secular society are not to shape the life of the church, and spiritual men are the ones called to ensure this.

Stated simply, godly men are charged to safeguard the godliness of the church. This responsibility starts with the elders but extends to all the men standing beside the elders to see that the Lord's church obeys the Lord's will. Godly men are to ensure that the church is a safe garden where the things of God are encouraged to flourish and the truth of God is upheld in faith.

Protect Church Doctrine

Godly men are especially to guard the doctrine of the church. Again, all the men, but particularly the elders, are to stand up for truth in this way. This is another affirmation of the Christian man's need to study to become sound in doctrine and to make himself aware of the current threats to truth. In our society today, these would include liberal assaults on the Bible and worldly compromises of what the Bible teaches.

If church leaders fail to uphold sound doctrine, godly men in the congregation should meet with them to exhort them to do so. If pastors and elders will not do so, faithful men should seek legitimate means of replacing them with other men who will faithfully serve the Lord. In some cases, a man may need to lead his family to another church. I cannot imagine how any Christian man could allow his family to join or remain in a church that is weak in doctrine, much less one that teaches falsely. Doctrine must take precedence above all matters of aesthetics or personal preferences. The style of music, demographics, the meeting place or architecture, or the personality of the minister, for example, are simply not as important as whether a church is preaching and teaching the Scriptures faithfully and accurately.

Jesus praised the church in Ephesus for properly testing its teachers (Rev. 2:2) and upbraided the church at Pergamum for failing to oust its false teachers (Rev. 2:15). Jude 1:3 urges us to "contend for the faith that was once for all delivered to the saints." If we do not guard the sacred trust of truth (2 Tim. 1:14), our wives and children will suffer under the spiritual bondage of error and lies.

The order God intends for the local church includes rich and valuable roles for women, as well. In healthy churches overseen by vigilant men, women can devote themselves to spreading the spiritual beauty for which they are designed and to nurturing the loving community and relationships in which they are intended to specialize. A strong, masculine church will also be a strong church for the display and fruitfulness of godly femininity. A church that is rightly run by godly men who know and apply the wholesome truths of God's Word is a safe church where women may blossom in the grace of the Lord.

BEHIND THE SCAFFOLDING

At a celebration of the 350th anniversary of the Westminster Confession of Faith, held at Westminster Abbey in London several years ago, the great Scottish preacher Eric Alexander spoke about Paul and the early Christians. Despite persecution and difficulty, these believers devoted themselves to building up local churches. Pastor Alexander pointed out that their knowledge of what God was doing in church history compelled them to the work and "injected a certainty into their tentative, weak, poor faith. It gave many of them a security in a desperately insecure world." The same could be said for the builder/guardians from Nehemiah's day, working so hard on a city that others had given up for lost, for they knew it to be part of God's unfailing project for salvation in the world. Pastor Alexander pointed out, "Were we more heavenly-minded in our living, it would do the same for us."[17]

Pastor Alexander went on to ask a series of pointed questions to make us think about our own lives. He asked,

What is the really important thing that is happening in the world in our generation? Where are the really significant events taking place? What is the most important thing? Where do you need to look in the modern world to see the most significant event from a divine perspective? Where is the focus of God's activity in history?

How would you answer those questions? What would you identify as the great work taking place in our world, the most interesting thing that demands our attention today? Pastor Alexander gave his answer:

> The most significant thing happening in history is the calling, redeeming, and perfecting of the people of God. God is building the church of Jesus Christ. The rest of history is simply a stage God erects for that purpose. He is calling out a people. He is perfecting them. He is changing them. History's great climax comes when God brings down the curtain on this bankrupt world and the Lord Jesus Christ arrives in his infinite glory. The rest of history is simply the scaffolding for the real work.[18]

Pastor Alexander finished by mentioning that the last time he had been in London, Westminster Abbey had been covered in scaffolding as workers were cleaning and beautifying it. "One could not see its true beauty," he noted, "but one was aware that something of great significance was happening behind that scaffolding. Something of majestic beauty was to be revealed." Drawing upon that image, he applied it to our lives and to the church:

> There will come a day when God will pull down the scaffolding of world history. Do you know what he will be pointing to when he says to the whole creation, "There is my masterpiece?" He will be pointing to the church of Jesus Christ. In the forefront of it all will be the Lord Jesus himself who will come and say, "Here

am I, and the children you have given me, perfected in the beauty of holiness."[19]

That is the day for which we are laboring now as men in the church. In times past, the Israelites under Nehemiah offered themselves for rebuilding that great city Jerusalem to which Jesus would one day come as the Savior of the world. In a later time, spreading out from that same city, Paul and the other early Christians faced down the hostility of the Roman empire with the power of truth and love as they built the earliest Christian churches and safeguarded God's deposit of saving truth. Now is the time for us. And like Nehemiah, Paul, and those who labored with them, we must fix our eyes on the day to which all our labor is directed, the day when we ourselves will be resurrected in glory and when God will fully manifest His splendor in His people. If we live for that day now, it will strengthen us to the work of building the church of Christ together, in His name and with His power, striving with all our might to safeguard the gospel, which gives the only hope of salvation to a world lost in sin.

Questions for Reflection and Discussion

- How clear is the Bible's teaching on male-only leadership in positions of teaching and authority? Does adherence to this requirement make a real difference in the life of a church? What are ways in which this requirement can be abused? What are ways in which ignoring it is harmful?

- Even if you are not now called to serve as an elder or deacon, how do the biblical requirements for these offices apply to your life as a Christian man? How can these guidelines serve to focus your spiritual growth?

- Do you believe that God has given you specific spiritual gifts that are to be used in the church? If so, what are they and how are you using them? If you are unsure about your gifts, how do you think you might learn what they are?

- In what ways do non-ordained Christian men play an important role alongside the elders and deacons? Do you think that your godliness matters in your church? How can you show leadership as a Christian man, whether you are ordained or not?

- Do you consider yourself to be sound in the faith? If not, how can you safeguard your family and church against error? What steps should you take to ensure that you know sound doctrine? If you consider yourself sound in the faith, what can you do to continue growing in your knowledge and to use your knowledge to benefit the church?

---- Chapter 13 ----

SERVANTS OF
THE LORD

There are many things I look forward to as a Christian man. I look forward to seeing my daughters marry godly young men (though how I will afford the weddings is a mystery). I look forward to reaching twenty years in the same pulpit, because I believe fruitfulness in ministry requires a long-term commitment to people and place. I look forward, should it please the Lord, to seeing one of my children ordained into the gospel ministry or commissioned as a full-time missionary. But far above all these events—none of which is certain—I look forward to an event that rises above every other. I look forward to meeting in person, and seeing with my own eyes, the Lord of glory, the Son of God, my Savior and Master, the King of kings, Jesus Christ.

Unlike the other things for which I hope, this glorious event is absolutely certain. As Job marveled, "I know that my Redeemer lives, and that in the end he will stand upon the earth. And after my skin has been destroyed, yet in my flesh I will see God. I myself will see him with my own eyes—I, and not another" (Job 19:25–27 NIV). Job then exclaimed, "My heart faints within me!" To this I say "Amen!" because these words are true for me, and they are true for you as well.

Many people, I realize, live and work with their eyes on retirement. Everything is thus measured by its contribution to the IRA or another retirement fund. But I believe a Christian man should live, work, and play with an eye on the coming glory of Jesus Christ. His return in glory is not a fable, a fantasy, or science fiction. It is certain future history—it *is* going to happen, and relatively soon. How should we then live? How should we measure things happening in our lives? The answer is that we should live now in the light of the future that is certain to come.

According to the Bible, there are rewards in heaven for our service to Christ on earth. This is why Jesus tells us to "lay up treasure in heaven" (Matt. 6:20) and why the parable of the ten minas shows the giving of differing rewards to servants with differing amounts of profit (Luke 19:17). I admit I have a hard time thinking of any reward greater than mere entrance into the glorious kingdom of our Lord. I will see him, and I imagine myself kneeling at his feet and worshiping His glory. Then I will hear words from His lips, the anticipation of which defines my entire present existence: "Well done, good and faithful servant. Enter into the joy of your master" (Matt. 25:21). This is the future event, the future reward, that should motivate every Christian to live in a bold and mighty way in service to Jesus Christ.

With this in mind, it does not matter whether I am successful as we measure things in this world. It does not matter if the world embraces or despises me. It does not matter if I abound or am abased. What matters is that I be found faithful and hear those words from Jesus Christ, my Savior and Master, the Lord who is coming again to reign forever. To be a Christian means not merely that I am saved from my sins, but also that I am saved to be His disciple. That is what Christian men are: followers, disciples, and servants of the Lord Jesus Christ. The certainty of His return, and His commendation of faithful men and women, is the great and colossal fact that should dominate our view of the future.

PERSONAL DISCIPLES OF CHRIST

A number of years ago, when I was still teaching at a college, some leaders from a well-known quasi-Christian cult came to see me. This is a group that demands to take over every aspect of your life. They made the statement that each Christian is to be a disciple. Although their definition of a Christian is fundamentally flawed, for the sake of discussion I was willing to agree with this statement. They then asked me if I was being personally discipled. To their surprise, I answered that I was. When they inquired as to who was discipling me, no doubt intending to express their disapproval, my answer was not what they expected. "I am being discipled by Jesus of Nazareth," I replied. "But He is dead and is no longer here," they demanded. "That is where you are wrong," I replied, "for He lives now and ministers to His believers through the Holy Spirit. As a true believer in

Jesus, I am a personal disciple to Him now, no less than Peter, John, and the others were His disciples when He walked upon the earth."

This answer exposed a common problem among ostensibly Christian cults, namely, the absence of a role for the Holy Spirit in their thinking and living (a role the cults seek to usurp in the lives of their followers). For it is through the ministry of the Holy Spirit that every Christian today truly is a personal disciple of Jesus. Not only is our discipleship *not inferior* to that of those who walked on the earth with our Lord, it is *better*. This is what Jesus said in His meeting with the disciples on the evening of His arrest: "I tell you the truth," Jesus said, "it is to your advantage that I go away, for if I do not go away, the Helper will not come to you. But if I go, I will send him to you" (John 16:7). No doubt every Christian has imagined how wonderful it would have been to live as a disciple of Jesus prior to His resurrection. But here, Jesus Himself said that the addition of the Helper, the Holy Spirit, makes for an even better discipleship.

To understand what it means to be a personal disciple and servant of the Lord Jesus is to rejoice and exult in that present privilege. Central to this service is making time to sit at His feet, learn from His Word, and speak with Him in prayer. Jesus said, "If you abide in my word, you are truly my disciples" (John 8:31). This means our discipleship is mere talk unless we are dwelling in God's Word and communing with the Lord in regular prayer. And why wouldn't we? For Jesus promises great results if we will be true disciples: "You will know the truth, and the truth will set you free" (John 8:32).

Marks of a true disciple of Jesus, someone set free by abiding in His truth, are demonstrated by John the Baptist. John spoke of his joy in serving One so great as Jesus, when he said, "He who is mightier than I is coming, the strap of whose sandals I am not worthy to untie" (Luke 3:16). Undoing the latch of a sandal was a task so menial and dirty that in ancient Judea even slaves were not required to do it. But John said that when it comes to serving Jesus, this lowest task was not merely *beneath him*—in reference to Jesus it was actually *far above him*, so great is the glory of the Son of God, our Lord.

Jesus regarded John the Baptist as the greatest person of the Old Testament (see Matt. 11:11). But John regarded himself as a personal servant of the Lord Jesus, seeing the slightest thing he might do for One so great as Jesus as the highest privilege and thrill he could ever imagine.

LIVING AS A SERVANT-DISCIPLE

If we want to make a difference with our lives by serving Jesus, we should adopt the attitude John the Baptist displayed. To this end, I would like to begin wrapping up this book on Christian manhood with the Baptist's teaching on the glory of serving Jesus as His disciple.

John 3:22–30 records a time during which John's ministry was diminishing in the light of Christ's growing fame, to the extent that John's followers had begun leaving him to follow Jesus instead. Some of John's still-devoted followers complained to him about the way Jesus' ministry was eclipsing John's. The Baptist's answer is a classic statement of godly faithfulness and a model for how Christian men may yield themselves unreservedly to the Lord:

> "A person cannot receive even one thing unless it is given him from heaven. . . . The one who has the bride is the bridegroom. The friend of the bridegroom, who stands and hears him, rejoices greatly at the bridegroom's voice. Therefore this joy of mine is now complete. He must increase, but I must decrease." (John 3:27, 29–30)

Here we have John's model of service to Christ. That model includes a *key principle,* a *joyful attitude,* and a *humble resolution.* Together, these elements can enable us as men to be faithful to our calling to carry out the Masculine Mandate in service to Christ.

Calling as a Gift: A Key Principle

First, in response to his followers who resented the growing prominence of Jesus, John set forth this key principle for serving the Lord: "A person cannot receive even one thing unless it is given him from heaven" (John 3:27). John's point was that men must content themselves with the place and provision the sovereign God gives them, seeking only to be faithful to one's particular calling.

Here is the antidote to jealousy and strife among Christians, for John's statement reminds us that everything we have is a gift from heaven. If we have great gifts and a great calling, they were given by God for His service. If we have modest gifts and a modest calling, these too were given by God for His service. Knowing this should keep us from the twin challenges of jealousy on the one hand and boasting on the other. Paul asks: "What do you have that you did not receive? If then you received it, why do you boast as if you did not receive it?" (1 Cor. 4:7). So if we have gifts, they came from God. If we are successful, it is because of God's grace. If we have been diligent, even that has been a heavenly gift. For this reason, we should not glorify those whom we see as successful Christians, but instead give all glory to God. Conversely, if God has granted us lesser success, we should not be envious of those who have more. All that we have comes from God and is for His glory.

This understanding helps us distinguish between godly and ungodly ambition. Yes, Christians are to be ambitious, but for the right things. We are to have energy and zeal for the kingdom of God. We should aspire to work and keep as Christians: to provide for those under our care, to do good in the world, to protect and nurture the weak, and especially to bring people to faith in Christ and disciple them to Christian maturity.

Whatever gifts you have, you should be ambitious about what God can make of them and do through them. Of course, this is a far cry from the selfish ambition that often comes so much more naturally to us. We tend to be most concerned with our reputation and well-being. This is where our envy and strife come from: we want to be glorified and admired—otherwise, why would we worry that others are more prominent than we are? We want to enjoy or acquire high position, riches, and worldly luxuries—if not, then why do we become anxious when these things are threatened? John's principle is key both for our usefulness to God and our spiritual well-being. If we can replace self-centered ambition with God-centered ambition, we will be free of envy and strife.

The gifted preacher F.B. Meyer struggled with envy. God called him to serve in London at the same time as Charles Haddon Spurgeon, arguably the greatest preacher who ever lived. So, despite his ability and hard work, Meyer would stand outside his church and watch the carriages flow by to Spurgeon's Metropolitan Tabernacle. Later in his life, it happened again, as G. Campbell Morgan eclipsed Meyer's success. When they spoke together at conferences, vast crowds listened to Morgan, then left when Meyer was to preach. Convicted over his bitter spirit, Meyer committed himself to pray for Morgan, reasoning that the Holy Spirit would not allow him to envy a man for whom he prayed. He was right. God enabled Meyer to rejoice in Morgan's preaching. People heard him saying: "Have you heard Campbell Morgan preach? Did you hear that message this morning? My, God is upon that man!"[20] In response to Meyer's prayers, Morgan's church so overflowed that people came and filled Meyer's church, too.

It is the glory of John the Baptist that he apparently had no such struggles when it came to Jesus. He knew that he was not the Savior: "You yourselves bear me witness, that I said, 'I am not the Christ, but I have been sent before him'" (John 3:28). John understood his place and role; all along he had been preparing and then directing people to follow Jesus, the true Lamb of God and Savior. Thus, he rejoiced when they did so. It did not bother him in the least that his star was declining with the rising light of Christ. God is sovereign, John knew. To each of us, God apportions works and the gifts to accomplish them. What matters is that we faithfully fulfill our particular calling to the glory of God, seeking His approval instead of man's praise.

This is one reason why understanding the Bible's mandate for men is so important. John said that he only wanted to fulfill what the Lord had decided for him to do. What has the Lord decided for you to do? What is your calling? For starters, you may be certain that you have the calling of Genesis 2:15—"The LORD God took the man and put him in the garden of Eden to work it and keep it." From the very roots of humanity and the first pages of Scripture, the essence of your calling and mine is clear. We are to work and keep in whatever corner of the kingdom God has placed us. Understanding and embracing this essential aspect of our calling is a key to living fruitfully as a servant-disciple of Christ.

Joy: A Key Attitude

The second great thing we note in John the Baptist is a by-product of the first and is itself a key to our faithfulness as Christians. John told his followers that, far from being frustrated by his waning prominence, he maintained a joyful attitude in his service to the Lord. "The one who has the bride is the bridegroom," John explained. "The friend of the bridegroom, who stands and hears him, rejoices greatly at the bridegroom's voice. Therefore this joy of mine is now complete" (John 3:29).

This "friend of the bridegroom" idea can make John's statement seem hard to grasp, but it doesn't have to be. In ancient Israel, this person was like a best man—but a best man with huge authority and responsibility, since he also served as the wedding planner, master of ceremonies, and security detail for the newlyweds' love nest:

> He acted as the liaison between the bride and the bridegroom; he arranged the wedding; he took out the invitations; he presided at the wedding feast. He brought the bride and the bridegroom together. . . . It was his duty to guard the bridal chamber and let no false lover in . . . when he heard the bridegroom's voice he let him in and went away rejoicing, for his task was completed and the lovers were together.[21]

For a while, this friend of the bridegroom would be in the spotlight. But all along, his purpose would be to serve the bride and groom, usher them safely into one another's arms, and then gladly and gracefully fade into the background. His joy came not from being seen, but from the privilege of performing his service, in the honor he showed to his friend, and in the sheer delight of bringing the bride and groom together.

As John first prepared the way for the Savior and then openly proclaimed Jesus when the Lord began His public ministry, John saw the re-direction of public attention away from himself and toward Jesus. John knew this was exactly the right thing at the right time, for his purpose was to use any visibility he might have (as a gift from God) to point to Christ. Seeing the successful completion of this most important task in his life, he was able to say, "Therefore this joy of mine is now complete."

James Montgomery Boice asks:

> Do you know that joy? Some persons think that there is great joy in material possessions, but things in themselves do not satisfy. Others think that there is joy in worldly fame, achievement, or pleasure, but these goals are relatively unrewarding. They satisfy at best for a short time. Real joy comes in being able to say to Jesus Christ, "Here I am, Lord, use me," and then finding that out of His grace He is able to use you to bring others into a saving relationship to Himself.[22]

What is the greatest reward for service to Jesus? It is simply the joy of serving Jesus. This joy makes us faithful and useful as servants of Christ. It enables us to rejoice not merely when our efforts are blessed with success, not merely when others praise and approve us, but whenever we have the privilege of serving Jesus, simply because of our love for Him and our awareness of how great He is.

John the Baptist was overwhelmed with the joy and privilege of doing anything—even unlatching a dirty sandal—for so great a Lord as Jesus Christ. So his joy was especially great when God used him to direct others to Jesus. Our joy in leading people toward Christ should be great as well. Our goal in evangelizing the lost and encouraging the saints is not to attain glory for ourselves. We do these things for the same reason the friend of the groom in ancient Israel brought to him his bride. We do it for our love of them both and the simple joy of serving the Lord.

Humility: A Key Resolution

Finally, in uttering what Leon Morris has described as "some of the greatest words ever to fall from the lips of mortal man,"[23] John revealed the third element of his service to Christ. Not only did John refuse to compete with Jesus or show envy toward Him. John went further and declared, "He must increase, but I must decrease" (John 3:30). That is, John not only accepted the change in public stature between him and Jesus that already had occurred, he embraced the acceleration and continuation of that process, resolving joyfully that his ministry must give way to that of Christ. In the same way, Christians who are useful and make a difference in this world are resolved to make little of themselves so that Christ will be exalted, believed, and followed.

This kind of humility does not come naturally, and the attitude John displays here is not an easy one to adopt. By nature, we always want our own stature to increase. Indeed, this self-exalting attitude is at the heart of all sin. The Serpent sealed the original temptation to sin by promising, "You will be like God" (Gen. 3:5). In reality, sin makes us like the Serpent—that is, Satan—whose constant desire is to increase in rebellion to God.

Yet John the Baptist models the highest godliness when he says, "I must decrease." To be humble is to be Christlike;

indeed, it is only in Christ that we can ever truly be humble. A.W. Pink rightly says:

> Humility is not the product of direct cultivation, rather it is a *by-product*. The more I try to be humble, the less shall I attain unto humility. But if I am truly occupied with that One who was "meek and lowly in heart," if I am constantly beholding His glory in the mirror of God's Word, then shall I be "changed into the *same image from* glory to glory, even as by the Spirit of the Lord" (2 Cor. 3:18).[24]

Humility is not a pathetic guise we wear because we must. Humility is a glorious grace that is a key to true greatness. The apostle Peter wrote, "Clothe yourselves, all of you, with humility toward one another, for 'God opposes the proud but gives grace to the humble'" (1 Peter 5:5). A.W. Tozer comments:

> True humility is a healthy thing. The humble man accepts the truth about himself. He believes that in his fallen nature dwells no good thing. He acknowledges that apart from God he is nothing, has nothing, knows nothing and can do nothing. But this knowledge does not discourage him, for he knows also that in Christ he is somebody. He knows that he is dearer to God than the apple of His eye and that he can do all things through Christ who strengthens him; that is, he can do all that lies within the will of God for him to do. . . . When this belief becomes so much a part of a man that it operates as a kind of

unconscious reflex . . . the emphasis of his life shifts from self to Christ, where it should have been in the first place, and he is thus set free to serve his generation by the will of God without the thousand hindrances he knew before.[25]

This is why God's greatest servants have all been humble people. Moses was the great deliverer of the Old Testament, and the Bible calls him "very meek, more than all people who were on the face of the earth" (Num. 12:3). It was as a humble servant that David was called "a man after God's own heart" (1 Sam. 13:14). John the Baptist, whom Jesus called the greatest mortal man yet born, declared, "He must increase; I must decrease." And above them all towers the Lord Jesus Christ, who said, "Come to me, all who labor and are heavy laden, and I will give you rest. . . . For I am gentle and lowly in heart, and you will find rest for your souls" (Matt. 11:28–29).

BEHOLD, THE BONDSERVANT OF THE LORD

I began this book with a story about Brian Deegan—a hardcore motorcyclist who converted to Christianity—whom I first read about in a sports magazine while sitting in a barber shop (*not* a hair salon). Having thus established my masculine credentials from page one, I'm perfectly comfortable comparing myself, here at the end of this book, to a young woman who inspires me to be a faithful servant of Christ.

The young woman is Mary, Jesus' mother. Here she is, a teenage girl living in what is morally a rather conservative religious culture. Betrothed to be married, and thus expected by everyone to be a virgin, she is visited by an angel, who tells her, "The Holy Spirit will come upon you, and the power of the Most High will overshadow you; therefore the child to be born will be called holy—the Son of God. . . . For nothing will be impossible with God" (Luke 1:35, 37). On its face, this is all rather incredible and disturbing. It is disturbing because it means she will be obviously pregnant before her wedding. It is incredible because of the messenger—an angel—and the essence of his message: that this seemingly suspicious pregnancy will result in the birth of Israel's long-promised Savior.

I see this young woman, our sister in the faith, receiving instructions that are simply staggering. She might well complain, weep, object, or flee. Instead, she bows her head and declares to God, "Behold, I am the servant of the Lord; let it be to me according to your word" (Luke 1:38).

If this is how a teenage female believer, indwelt by the Holy Spirit, can answer God's call to faithfulness, then so can we as Christian men! God calls us to bear His image in the world, both in the kind of men we are and in the labor we enter on His behalf. Surely we can answer, "Behold, we men are your servants, Lord."

God placed man in the garden, just as He now sovereignly places us into covenant relationships and specific life situations. The Lord tells us "to work it and keep it," so that in joyful obedience we may serve Him by building up, nurturing, and cultivating for growth, while also keeping and guarding so that all that is under our care is kept safe. It is a simple calling in that it is easy to understand, but it is not often easy to live.

God calls us to love our wives, to disciple and discipline our children, to be faithful in friendship, and to be zealous in the work of His kingdom. The great calling of our lives is to answer: "Behold, I am your servant, Lord. Help me by your grace to be faithful to your call."

May God raise up a host of such men in our time, and may we kneel before our sovereign Lord, seeking His grace, and declare to Him: "Lord, I receive my gifts and my calling from You. My great joy is to serve so great a Lord as You. I humble myself to work and keep so that Jesus may be exalted in my life. Behold, Your servant, Lord." If we will do that, answering the Lord's call on our lives in trusting faith, we can be sure that our Savior God will give us the grace needed to serve and lead as the gospel men He calls us to be. Then, when the muster roll of the saints is called at last in heaven, we may expectantly look forward to hearing the Lord say to us the words that Christian men should prize above all others: "Well done, good and faithful servant. Enter into the joy of your Master" (Matt. 25:21).

Questions for Reflection and Discussion

- Do you often think about the return of our Lord Jesus Christ? If not, what else in the future forms your thoughts about the present? Why is the second coming of Christ the great event that defines everything now?

- Do you think of yourself as a personal disciple of Jesus? If not, why don't you tend to think this way?

Are you helped by the discussion in this chapter of being Christ's disciple? How does the Holy Spirit minister to Christians now on Christ's behalf?

- What principle is mentioned in this chapter as key to Christian faithfulness? Have you ever struggled with envy toward other Christians? Why is this wrong and counterproductive? What is the remedy for envy and the key to godly ambition as a Christian man?

- The author states that the chief reward of serving Christ is the sheer joy of serving Christ. Do you agree? Have you experienced this joy? What happens when our service to Jesus is motivated by our pursuit of other rewards? Why should serving Jesus Christ be such an overwhelming joy to us, even in hardship?

- How do we become humble? How does humility make a difference in our service to the Lord? The author mentions Moses, David, and John the Baptist as examples of humility. Can you think of things in their lives that show humility? Can you think of ways in which Jesus is "lowly and meek," as He says He is? Is it manly to seek such a description?

- Jesus promises to greet all His faithful servants with the words "Well done." What does this prospect mean to you? Pray about how you might live now so as to hear those words when Jesus returns.

Notes

1 Cited in Chris Palmer, "Reinventing the Wheel," in *ESPN The Magazine* 11.15 (July 28, 2008), 52–58.

2 Accessed online at http://etnies.com/blog/2008/12/19/real-deal-deegan/.

3 John Eldredge, *Wild at Heart: Discovering the Secret of a Man's Soul* (Nashville, Tenn.: Thomas Nelson, 2001), 3.

4 Ibid., 4.

5 Bruce K. Waltke, *Genesis: A Commentary* (Grand Rapids, Mich.: Zondervan, 2001), 87.

6 The material in this section is drawn from my book *The Heart of an Executive* (New York: Doubleday, 1999), 5–7.

7 In the case of many men, a problem is unbiblical expectations that limit the pool of women to whom they are attracted. For biblical counsel on this important topic, readers might consider chapter 5 in the dating book my wife and I wrote, *Holding Hands, Holding Hearts: Recovering a Biblical View of Christian Dating* (Phillipsburg, N.J.: P&R, 2006).

8 John Calvin, *Genesis* (Edinburgh, Scotland: Banner of Truth Trust, 1847, reprint 1992), 129.

9 Victor P. Hamilton, *The Book of Genesis, Chapters 1–17* (Grand Rapids, Mich.: Eerdmans, 1990), 191.

10 In this chapter, I am assuming that a Christian man's wife is herself a Christian. The Bible makes clear we are not to marry non-Christians (1 Cor. 7:39), although when a man is converted after marrying, his wife may remain in unbelief. Nevertheless, the biblical teaching in this chapter will provide a valuable model for the husband even of a non-Christian wife.

11 Ted Tripp, *Shepherding a Child's Heart* (Wapwallopen, Pa.: Shepherd, 1995), 105.

12 Ibid., 107.

13 Some commentators argue that the biblical emphasis on "the rod" indicates that we should not spank with our own hands but should

use a suitable implement—a large spoon, for instance—to spank our children. The idea may be for the child not to think of the father's hand as a source of fear.

14 Dietrich Bonhoeffer, *Life Together* (San Francisco: Harper & Row, 1954), 23.

15 Some scholars argue that the use of the term *servant* to describe some women in the New Testament epistles indicates that they held the office of deacon, since the same word is used both to describe an unordained servant and an ordained deacon. The problem with this view is that Paul's description of the qualifications stipulates male-only eligibility ("husband of one wife" is used for both elders and deacons, 1 Tim. 3:2, 12) and also that the general term *servant* is also used by Paul for non-Christians, such as the emperor (Rom. 13:4). A sound treatment of the New Testament qualifications for offices shows that the general use of the term deacon/servant can be applied to anyone, including women and non-Christians, whereas the official use of this term for deacons is specifically restricted to men.

16 These lists also include some gifts that properly belong only to the apostolic age, such as miracles and prophecy.

17 Eric Alexander, "The Application of Redemption," in *To Glorify and Enjoy God: A Commemoration of the 350th Anniversary of the Westminster Assembly,* ed. John L. Carson and David W. Hall (Edinburgh, Scotland: Banner of Truth, 1994), 245.

18 Ibid.

19 Ibid., 245–246.

20 R. Kent Hughes, *John* (Wheaton, Ill.: Crossway, 1999), 95.

21 William Barclay, *The Gospel of John* (Philadelphia: Westminster, 1975), 1:143–44.

22 James Montgomery Boice, *The Gospel of John* (Grand Rapids, Mich.: Baker, 1999), 1:257.

23 Leon Morris, *The Gospel According to John* (Revised), New International Commentary on the New Testament (Grand Rapids, Mich.: Eerdmans, 1995), 118.

24 Arthur W. Pink, *Exposition of the Gospel of John* (Grand Rapids, Mich.: Zondervan, 1975), 149.

25 A.W. Tozer, *God Tells the Man Who Cares*, ed. Anita Bailey (Camp Hill, Pa.: Christian Publications, 1970), 138–40.

Index of Scripture

Index of Subjects and Names

About the Author

Richard D. Phillips (M.Div., Westminster Theological Seminary; D.Div., Greenville Presbyterian Theological Seminary) is senior minister of the Second Presbyterian Church in Greenville, S.C., a member of the board and the council of the Alliance of Confessing Evangelicals, a member of the council of the Gospel Coalition, and a member of the board of trustees of Westminster Theological Seminary in Philadelphia.

He is the author of more than twenty-five books, including *Jesus the Evangelist, What's So Great about the Doctrines of Grace?* and *Hebrews* in the Reformed Expository Commentary series, for which he serves as coeditor.

Prior to his calling to the gospel ministry, Dr. Phillips served as a tank officer in the U.S. Army and was assistant professor of leadership at the United States Military Academy at West Point, resigning with the rank of major.